FOREWORD

Classroom art 5–7 is a compilation of art activities to inspire students to communicate through visual arts and aid their development as young artists. The activities provide opportunities for directed skill development in the disciplines of drawing, painting and printmaking, while remaining largely open-ended, encouraging students to experiment and explore the possibilities of using their own unique techniques and ideas. The activities cover the use of a wide range of inexpensive media readily available in craft stores and schools and stimulate imagination by building from familiar ideas to an individual response.

Information to support the teacher includes:

- step-by-step pictorial instructions,

- ideas for inspiring the students,

- examples of finished artworks to use as a student stimulus,

- response questions to assist the students to analyse and appraise the skills used, the elements of art (line, shape, colour, pattern and texture) and the content of their own artwork and the artworks of others,

- variations and stimulus to provoke invention upon each activity,

- cross-curricular activity suggestions, and

- display suggestions.

Published 2004

RIC – 774
ISBN 978-1-74126-107-3

CONTENTS

About this book

DEVELOPING AWARENESS

The activities within *Classroom art* 5–7 will assist teachers in extracting an artistic response from students. This response will take a variety of forms as the students develop a deepening awareness of art's possibilities.

Art:

• encourages imagination and the ability to solve problems and work within set parameters,

• provides opportunity for lateral and original thought where there are no boundaries dictated by what is 'right' or 'wrong' but simply by what is possible,

• provides a rare vehicle through which we can directly or indirectly communicate and make personal statements about who we are and the life we are living.

To understand and create art, both as a skill and a human response, students need to be aware of the way art is composed. By providing students with a broad cross-section of activities, the teacher will be equipped to introduce and explore each of the 'elements of art' that combine to form visual arts. These elements of art include:

• line,

• shape,

• colour,

• pattern, and

• texture.

Exposure to and opportunities to exercise these elements, will provide students with the building blocks used by them and other artists to create images, project ideas and illusions, and describe atmosphere or 'tone' within an artwork. By developing artistic awareness in this way, students will be equipped to offer their own response with increased sensitivity.

ENCOURAGING CREATIVITY

In order to encourage creativity, the focus needs to be on individualism. All children make their own art in their own way. Art is one of the only disciplines where we are not required to compete against one another. In fact, the essence of producing art is in acquiring and demonstrating a different personal response – not the 'right' answer. Art is therefore something that everyone should participate in without fear.

However, students are often reluctant to participate in artistic activities for fear of producing substandard work. Because artwork is 'displayed', students may be left feeling exposed by their artwork. It is a good idea to start with more abstract styles to allow the students to build confidence in their ability to combine the elements of art in an informal way. Exposure to postmodern artists and their work can also develop awareness that art is a means of expression through the art elements, colour, shape, line, pattern and texture, rather than a means of replicating an image. Though every artwork a student produces may not 'work', it can be viewed as part of a process towards creating a work that is pleasing. Students need to be aware that sometimes things don't 'look' right, but that their awareness of what looks 'good' demonstrates their artistic ability and can be used to guide future efforts. It is often through these 'mistakes' that new inventive techniques, ideas and effects are born.

After making art, the students should talk about their work and become aware of why they have created it in the way they have. Many students will be content to look at their artwork and the artwork of others purely aesthetically. Encourage them to consider whether they have used their art to tell a story or show how they feel. By considering the purpose of their artwork as a means of sharing something of themselves or what they think or believe, many students can be encouraged to see their own work and the work of others as valuable, and be inspired to reach their true potential.

MODELLING

Students who are told to draw something with no prior practice or information merely repeat the symbols they always draw. Modelling plays an integral role in developing confidence in new artists and providing them with the tools they need to broaden their artistic response. Art does not simply 'explode' onto a page. There are basic skills and techniques involved, just as with any discipline, which require teaching and practice. It is by applying these skills and techniques to new situations and adapting them to suit the needs of the artist, that the individuality and creativity of art can be expressed.

Step-by-step pictorial instructions accompany each of the activities in *Classroom art* 5–7. These instructions provide teachers with a simple, logical process to follow and direct their students. A larger photo of a finished artwork has been included as a standard stimulus for the students to aspire to, but not necessarily as a model to copy.

Each artwork in the book aims to develop a different skill or technique or addresses and explores a new concept or style. The purpose of each activity has been described under 'Indications' and should be made clear to the students prior to the lesson and reviewed during the modelling process as a focus for the students to practise and develop.

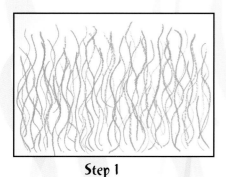

Step 1

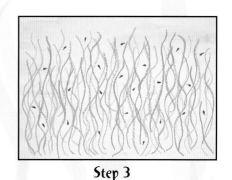

Step 2

Step 3

Step-by-step instructions – 'Tadpole pond', pp 16–17.

DEVELOPING SKILLS AND ENCOURAGING PRACTICE

Students love the success experienced by repeating and refining newly-learnt skills. Drawing, painting and printmaking techniques are no exception. It is often during skills-based activities that less confident art students will produce their most pleasing work and be inspired to branch out into more expressive ventures.

To be able to draw in different ways, students need to continue to explore drawing media in order to understand and use them for the special effects they wish to achieve. Allow the students time for 'discovery'. In practice sessions, include an element of exploration and an opportunity to develop a personal style. Challenge them with simple problem-solving tasks. For example, how many different types of marks can be made with a single media? How many more can be created using two media? Can you create marks to represent different textures – spiky, crinkly, swirly, muddy or rough? Can you invent a new colour by mixing paints and what would you name it? What other tools can be used to apply paint? Provide the students with a broad range of media to explore, and apply them to a variety of surfaces. When developing new skills, allow the students plenty of time to create so they can gain skills by looking, sharing ideas and practising.

Often, students will spontaneously create a picture while practising new techniques. These artworks should be valued and used to demonstrate that art is a composition of art elements – not necessarily a recognisable picture. Encourage students to share and discuss these artworks in terms of both content and the skills or techniques they used to create an effect that pleases them.

Practising spirals – 'Snail doodles', pp 6–7.

APPRAISING ART

Appraising art is a skill requiring an ability to look at art with personal criteria in mind. In this way, appraisals will vary from one person to another and cannot be assessed as 'right or wrong'. Initially, students will appraise work instinctively, using a 'what looks good' criterion. As they develop an understanding of the elements of art and how they interact to form a balanced image, these too will become part of their criteria. Older students will also address moods, medium, technique appropriateness, content and the artist's purpose in their appraisals. By using these criteria, students will learn to address what kind of art it is, why it has been made, what it is about, what materials or media have been used, and what techniques and art elements have been incorporated. Appraising the work of others – peers, older students, local and famous artists – helps students identify why and how we make art.

It is equally important for the students to appraise their own work in this way and to share their work with others. Encourage the students to focus on what they have done, the materials and tools used, what they have learnt, and what could be done better next time. Address what elements of art are in their work, and why they are or are not happy with their artwork. Be aware, though, that it is also acceptable not to discuss our own work. Sometimes our art is just for us.

CLASSROOM ORGANISATION

The environment in which the students create their artwork needs to be a balance of stimulation and organisation. A room with plenty of stimulus, artworks created by other artists and students, bright colours and elaborate displays, will inspire the students to stretch the boundaries of their ideas. However, a room that is too busy may crowd the students' thinking and prevent them from developing their own ideas, as so many are already on show to choose from. An environment that is neatly presented with stimulating displays is most effective. A well-presented workspace will also encourage the students to take pride in their personal work area and participate more readily in cleaning-up tasks.

Areas used for art can quickly become disaster areas. There should be a designated place for art media, brushes and tools, water containers with broad heavy bases, palettes, paper and cleaning equipment. Ensure the students know these places and are made responsible for their care. In this way, the students will be more particular and conservative with their use of valuable resources.

Ensure the students have their own painting shirt and that there is a ready supply of 'spares' for those that do not have one. A rubbish bag with head and armholes cut out makes an excellent makeshift painting shirt. Always insist upon the students wearing their painting shirts while cleaning up, as this is where most accidental drips and hand prints take place. Before messy art activities, cover the work surface with newspaper, which can be thrown away afterwards, or invest in cheap plastic drop sheets to use as cover-ups. Buckets with damp sponges, dry rags and soda water (for getting paint stains out of carpet and clothing) should also be on hand during messy activities, ready for unexpected spills.

SAFETY

Some art techniques and processes require the use of materials such as bleach and lit candles that may be harmful to the students if used incorrectly. Using these materials with lower primary students is not recommended. They should only be used in closely supervised situations with older students or adult assistance. Potentially dangerous materials have not been used in any activities in *Classroom art* 5–7.

Many art and craft media are toxic or lead-based and care should be taken when ordering or purchasing art supplies to ensure that they are non-toxic and safe for small children.

Supervision is essential when students are using scissors or any sharp tools. Blunt-ended scissors are recommended for younger, inexperienced users. Risk will be greatly reduced by modelling the correct use of scissors for the students prior to the activity.

The most common occurrences of accidents and injury are during the cleaning-up process. Provide a closely monitored, controlled environment in which the students can conduct cleaning tasks safely.

Activities involving materials such as bleach should be undertaken in well-ventilated areas.

PARENTAL INVOLVEMENT

Any activity involving young students will be more successful if adequate adult help is available. Parents are an invaluable part of classroom organisation. Establish a group of willing parents to become regulars with art activities. Orientate them with classroom organisation and clean up procedures. Allocate a number of students to each adult. Ask helpers to assist in providing and maintaining their group's resources, review instructions with the students and accompany them to designated clean-up tasks. Encourage the parents to create their own art if they would like to, and to model their thought process as they create. Always make a point of showing appreciation for parents who have taken time out to assist you and your students.

ASSESSMENT

Assessment of artworks created by students must be objective and the criteria by which they will be assessed made clear to the students before they create their artwork. Students must also be given the opportunity to reflect upon and discuss their own artwork and the artwork of others in order to demonstrate their understanding of art.

Ideally, assessment of visual arts should be made in four areas:

- ability to identify and discuss art ideas,

- demonstration of art skills, techniques and processes,

- response to visual arts through reflection and evaluation, and

- understanding the role of visual arts in society.

To evaluate a student's understanding and ability as an artist comprehensively, teachers may need to make use of a range of assessment tools, including observations, discussion transcripts and the artworks themselves. An art portfolio can be initiated and built over time to include examples of the student's developing skills, artistic responses and photos of finished pieces. The students will enjoy reflecting upon earlier artworks and monitoring their own development.

DISPLAY IDEAS

Classroom art displays can be used to create an atmosphere to enhance learning and encourage an awareness of how the elements of art, such as colour and pattern, can affect us and reflect the world around us. Clear, vibrant presentation will bring professionalism to the students' work and add value to their art.

Displays can be enhanced using materials in colours that support the artwork. Colours associated with the art's theme, simple frames set against a stark black background, or the use of many shades of one colour to increase vibrancy, are some methods used to enhance an artwork. Positioning the display in a prominent position in the room or using focused lighting will also add effect.

When developing a class display, involve the students in the process. Discuss whether the finished display looks good or how it could be made to look better, how it is positioned and how the art has been spaced, whether the background is appropriate and enhances the artwork, whether the mounts distract the eye from the art, what additions could be made to bring meaning to the art, or what text could be added.

Individual students' work can also be made a focus for display. By incorporating an 'artwork of the week' into the room, students can be encouraged to appraise their own art and learn to listen to others as they discuss their work and ask questions. When selecting a 'picture of the week', discuss why the picture was chosen and put up a sign describing the work and the reasons it was chosen.

Class display – 'Insect blots', pp 68–69.

UNDERSTANDING THE COLOUR WHEEL

Understanding colours, the effects they can create when placed against each other and how they mix to create new colours, is integral to creating pleasing artwork and displays. The following is an outline of the 'basics' of colour.

Primary colours

– yellow, blue, red.

Primary colours can be mixed to create all other base colours except black and white.

Tints

– adding white

Tints can be created by adding white to any base colour. Tints are commonly referred to as 'pastel' colours. Large quantities of white are required to significantly tint a base colour.

Shades

– adding black

Shades can be created by adding black to any base colour. Small quantities of black paint are required to make a base colour significantly darker.

Secondary colours

– green, orange, purple.

Secondary colours are created when two primary colours are mixed.

red + yellow = orange
yellow + blue = green
blue + red = purple

By adding more of one primary colour than the other, variations of a secondary colour can be made. For example, a small amount of yellow and a large amount of blue will make a blue-green colour. Adding black or white to two primary colours will create tints and shades of secondary colours.

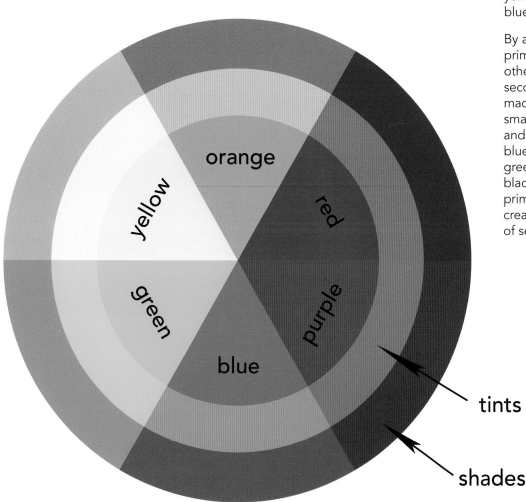

Tertiary colours

are created when any combination of three primary colours is mixed together.

When all three primary colours are mixed, variations of brown can be achieved by adding more or less of each colour. A chocolate brown colour can be made by combining equal parts of red and yellow and a very small amount of blue.

Complementary colours

are those which are opposite on the colour wheel and which stand out strongly when placed against one another. Examples of complementary colours are orange and blue, green and red and purple and yellow.

Analogous colours

Analogous colours describe those that exist side by side on the colour wheel. Artworks in analogous colours are generally composed in variations of two or three colours found side by side on the colour wheel; for example, blue, green and yellow.

RESOURCES

Colour media

lead pencil
coloured pencils
greasy crayons
fluorescent crayons
metallic crayons
felt-tipped pens
marking pens
black fine-tipped pen
acrylic paints
fluorescent paints
powdered tempera paint
edicol powder (dye)
food colouring

Other resources

foil
strong glue
ruler
toothpicks
paintbrush (large flat)
newspaper
scissors
coloured paper squares
sticky tape
textured papers
white art paper
templates or stencils
coloured mounting card
cornflour
soap flakes
mixing bowl
electric mixer
cooking salt
squeeze bottles
glass or plastic sheeting
detergent
liquid starch
coloured paper scraps
straw
glitter
sponges
toothbrushes
icing sugar
comb
fork
scrubbing brush
large flat tray
vegetables
green crepe paper
vegetation
small bowls
marbles
clay
envelopes
carving tools
textured fabric scraps
hard roller
candles
bubble wrap
sponge roller
steel wool
egg rings
kitchen scrubbers
feathers
fur off-cuts

INDICATIONS

Indications specific to each activity are provided. Each covers one of the following areas:

- skills, techniques and processes, and
- responding, reflecting on and evaluating visual arts.

SEEKING INSPIRATION

We are surrounded by stimuli. Becoming inspired to transform a stimulus into art requires a process by which the stimulus is sparked into an original idea worthy of expressing. This process may take place simply through quiet thought where a mental 'domino effect' will lead a simple stimulus to a different creative level.

However, in a classroom situation, it is often through discussion with others that original ideas are triggered. Therefore, for most art students, discussion is valuable and should not be discouraged.

Students should be encouraged to discuss why the pictures we draw or paint are different from photographs, to compare illustration styles, and the difference between real and abstract pictures. Students should also be encouraged to attempt to replicate the techniques used by other artists, watch artists work and to discuss art with artists themselves.

Teachers should expose the students to artworks that they are enthusiastic about themselves, and demonstrate a broad selection of styles and periods. This will provide discussion opportunities relating to specific artists, styles or movements, content, media and art elements; all of which provide key material from which students can develop interest and artistic direction.

Discussion, personal experiences and exposure to collections of art stimuli relating to a particular theme or style will provide a range of ideas for students to mesh into a new and unique idea for their own artwork.

Collections may include artworks or displays from other classrooms, prints, pictures in books, photographs, tools and media, photos, magazine articles, posters, artefacts, everyday objects, journal entries, poems, and other artists' work.

Each activity within *Classroom Art 5–7* is prefaced by a list of ideas that can be used to inspire student interest in readiness for the activity.

INSTRUCTIONS

Specific four-step instructions are given for each activity, with accompanying photographs.

REFLECTION QUESTIONS encourage students to evaluate the skills, techniques and processes used and extend students' thoughts concerning the use of the technique or subject, in order to appraise their art.

VARIATIONS

When students are using new techniques or responding to a new stimulus, there will always be opportunities for numerous variations on a theme. These variation activities will allow students to consolidate what they have learnt and will also demonstrate how a technique, idea or style can be altered to produce a different response. Students will often spontaneously see an opportunity for producing something unique from an activity, either prior to commencing or during the process of creating an artwork. Teachers should always allow the students to deviate and develop their creative response. There will be time for specific skill development later. Though technique is important, creativity should always take priority.

A list of suggested variations supplements each of the activities in *Classroom art 5–7*.

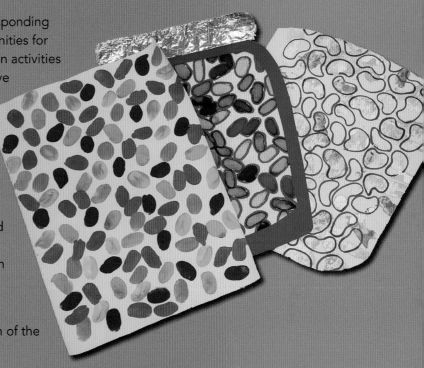

ACROSS THE CURRICULUM

Art is a wonderful means of expressing new discoveries and personal interests. Students learning new material in other curriculum areas will find art a stimulating means of expressing their new knowledge. Emersion within a theme or topic will provide ample stimulus for new and creative artwork. Although there is merit in teaching art in isolation for 'art's sake', in a classroom situation, student involvement in other areas of the curriculum can be utilised to form a foundation for original art ideas.

Each activity in *Classroom art 5–7* is accompanied by a list of suggested cross-curricular activities. These activities can be used to consolidate or complement learning in art lessons.

RECIPES FOR MEDIA

Liquid starch – Dissolve starch powder in a small amount of cold water to make a paste. Add boiling water, stirring continuously until the mixture becomes opaque and of the desired consistency. Create a thinner consistency for paint or a thicker consistency for use as a glue.

Liquid starch is suitable for gluing paper, sticks to metal, glass, waxed paper and plastic, and dries clear. Add edicol dye or powdered tempera paint to liquid starch to create a thicker, slightly translucent paint ideal for finger painting. Adding liquid starch to paint is an economical way to increase paint supplies and will keep for long periods in airtight containers in the refrigerator.

Cornflour paste – Use two tablespoons of cornflour to one cup of water. Mix enough water with the cornflour to make a paste. Add the remaining water and bring to the boil. Continue to stir until a custard-like consistency is achieved. Add water if a thinner consistency is preferred. Mix powdered tempera paints or edicol dye with a small amount of water and add to the mixture when cool.

Cornflour paste is suitable for gluing paper or for adding to edicol or powdered paint.

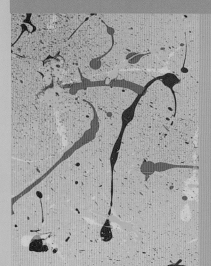

Edicol paint – Dissolve about $\frac{1}{8}$ of a teaspoon of edicol dye powder in a tablespoon of water and add to cornflour paste, commercially available wallpaper paste or liquid starch to create thick translucent paint in brilliant colours. Add detergent to the mixture to assist in adhesion to glass, plastics and foil. Mix edicol powder with small amounts of water to create vivid dyes for use on fabric or paper. Food colouring can be used as an inexpensive, but less vivid, substitute for edicol dye.

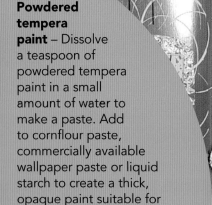

Powdered tempera paint – Dissolve a teaspoon of powdered tempera paint in a small amount of water to make a paste. Add to cornflour paste, commercially available wallpaper paste or liquid starch to create a thick, opaque paint suitable for covering patterned surfaces, such as lettering on boxes.

Soap paint – Pour two cups of warm water into a bowl. Using an electric mixer, begin mixing, adding soap flakes gradually. Beat until the soap forms soft peaks. Add colouring to the soap and mix through. Powdered tempera paint, edicol paint or acrylic paint can be used to colour soap paint successfully.

DRAWING

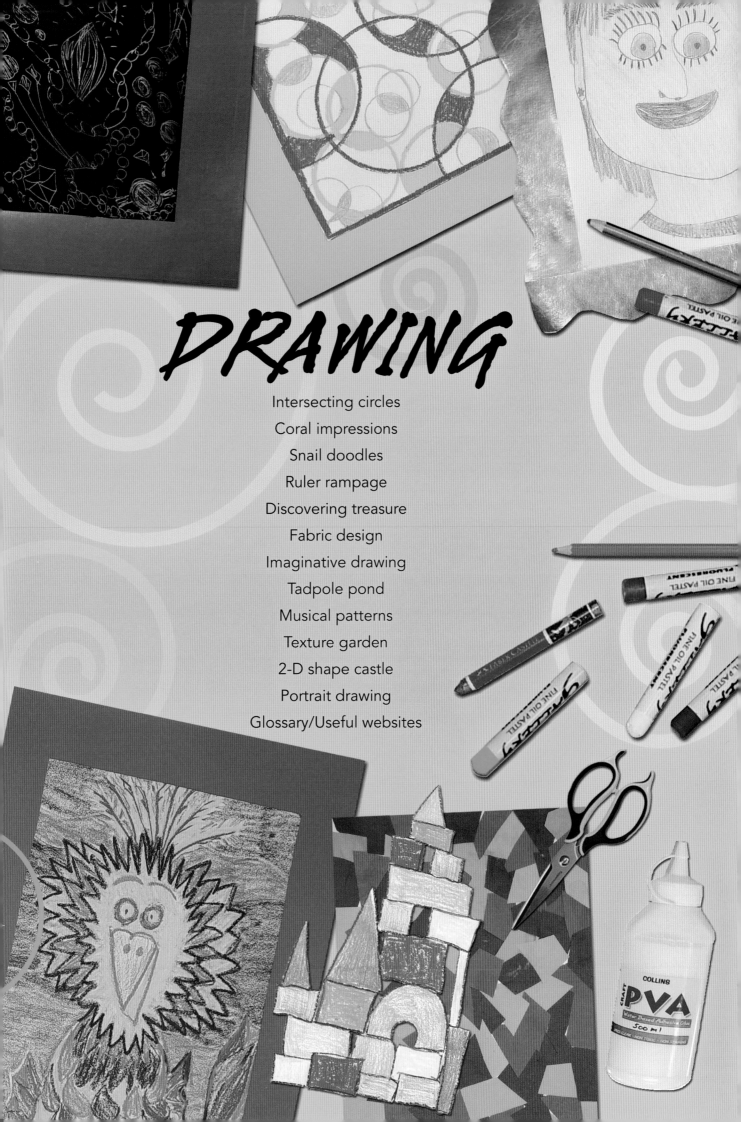

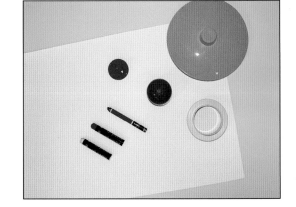

Resources

- yellow card for mounting
- yellow, orange and gold crayons
- 3 circular objects
- white paper

Indications:

Skills, techniques, technologies and processes

- Traces accurately around a circular template.
- Selects areas for colouring according to self-determined criteria.

Responding, reflecting on and evaluating visual arts

- Appreciates the vibrancy of colour produced by crayons as opposed to other drawing media.
- Discusses own artwork during its progress and suggests how it could be changed or improved.

Inspiration

- Draw circles in a variety of places; in sand, in the air, on paper.
- Blow bubbles and note their transparency.
- Discuss things in the sky that are round.
- Have the students suggest colours suitable for drawing a sun.
- Give the students opportunities to draw circular shapes which overlap, and identify the overlapping portion.

Instructions

Step 1

Select the largest of the circular objects. This will be the first template. Hold the template securely on the page using one hand and carefully trace around it using an orange crayon in the other. Some students may require an adult to help them hold their object initially, especially larger objects.

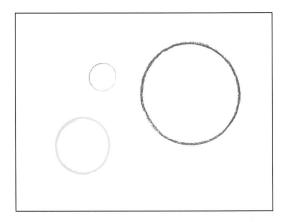

Step 2

Repeat Step 1 until four or five large circles have been traced onto the page in orange crayon. These circles may or may not overlap, depending on the wishes of the individual students. Select the middle-sized circle and the yellow crayon and trace around it up to 10 times, randomly across the page. The students should be encouraged to overlap the circles where they can without 'cluttering' the page or having too many circles in one area. Select the smallest circle to trace, and the gold crayon, and again trace many times with overlapping. There should be more of the smallest circles than the middle-sized circles on the page. Encourage the students to think about where they are placing each circle to avoid overcrowding.

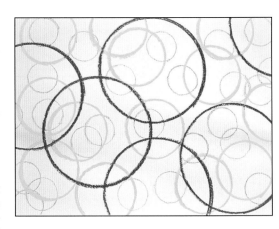

Step 3

Demonstrate what is meant by 'overlapping' by colouring an overlapped section on a diagram. Students select sections of the orange circles which are overlapping and colour them orange. They can then colour sections of the yellow circles in yellow and sections of the gold circles gold accordingly. If the students would like to colour their circles following their own system, this should be encouraged and the students asked to explain their colouring system to you or their peers.

Step 4 If desired, the background of the drawing (the area where no circles have been drawn) may be coloured orange or black. Choose a bright sheet of coloured card, such as yellow or orange, to mount the student's work. The drawings may be incorporated into a display about coins, shapes or summer. If used as a shape display, the students could be allowed, in future activities, to choose their own shape to represent.

Reflection questions

- Can you point to places where your circles overlap?
- Did you spread your circles out across the page evenly? Or are some circles bunched together? What looks better, bunched up or spread out?
- Why did you colour the sections that you did? Why did you choose particular colours for particular overlapping sections? Did you follow a special system of colouring?
- Would this activity work well for other shapes? What shapes do you think would be good to use?

Variations

- Use the same techniques to consolidate any new shape learnt.
- Use a template or stencil of a familiar object or animal.
- Draw several different regular or irregular shapes and colour the overlapping portions.
- Cut out several circles from different coloured cellophane and glue them down so that they overlap to create new colours.

Cross-curricular activities

- Locate circular objects around the room.
- Play games where the students need to participate by forming a circle.
- Group attribute blocks according to one or two given criteria.
- Become familiar with a variety of two-dimensional shapes.
- Identify three-dimensional shapes that roll.
- Play ball games.
- Introduce simple Venn diagrams.

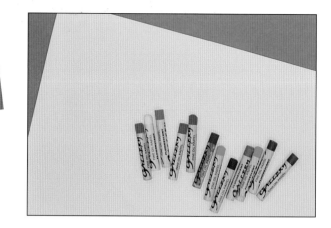

Resources
- fluorescent crayons
- white paper
- aqua card for mounting

Indications:

Skills, techniques, technologies and processes

- Uses crayons to create patterns with dots.
- Creates shapes using dots to represent a familiar object.

Responding, reflecting on and evaluating visual arts

- Enjoys creating a colourful image using dots.
- Appreciates the iridescent quality of fluorescent media.

Inspiration

- View impressionist paintings such as *The circus*, by Seurat (1891), where dots have been used to describe an image.
- View Aboriginal Australian artworks which are comprised of dots.
- Compare fluorescent colours to normal colours. Describe how the colours are the same but different.

Instructions

Step 1

Students choose a single colour to draw imaginary coral shapes using dots. It may help to show the students actual coral, noting its 'dotty', bumpy texture and allowing the students to feel the 'dots'. Encourage the students to make sure they leave a small gap between each dot to avoid the dots becoming messy.

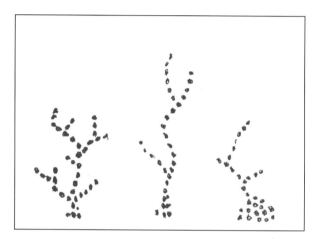

Step 2

Add other colours, using the initial colour as a base pattern around which to layer the others. These will become new coral formations. Encourage the students to think about the colours they are putting side by side and to attempt to 'balance' their drawing by keeping the design and spacing even across the page, rather than one area being heavier than the other.

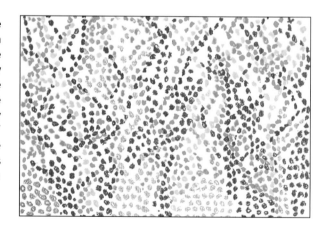

Step 3

Students choose a favourite colour as the dominant 'fill' colour. Add this colour to the drawing by using it to 'fill in' gaps, using smaller dots if necessary. This will help to accentuate the patterns they created using other colours.

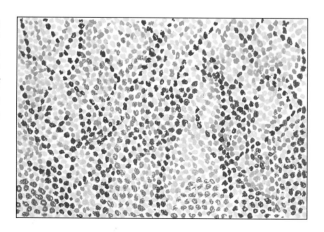

Coral impressions

Step 4 Trace around the drawing in a colour other than the 'dominant' colour chosen in Step 3. Mount the coral artwork on to 'sea'-green or blue card. The artwork can be further enhanced by a weak blue-green wash to hide any remaining white paper.

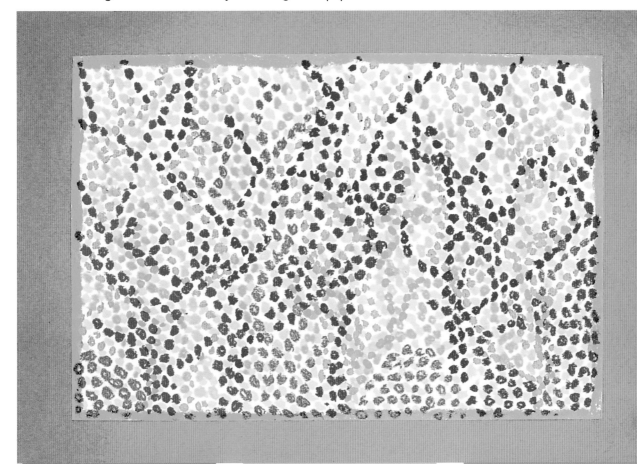

Reflection questions

- Can you tell what your picture is meant to be? Are the dots too muddled?
- What is your favourite colour? Did you use that colour a lot? Did it change the way your picture looked?
- What other pictures would look good using fluorescent colours?

Variations

- Use dots to make an unusual border for other drawings.
- Make concentric and radiating dot patterns and form dots in arrays.
- Paint over dot pictures drawn in greasy or waxy crayon with a colour wash to enhance the iridescent quality of the crayon.

Cross-curricular activities

- Find out about coral and reefs.
- Discuss how coral looks and feels like a rock but is actually made by living things.
- Make lists of living and nonliving things found in rock pools.
- Write a narrative told by a coral polyp about an underwater adventure it has had.

Resources
- black card for mounting
- pastel green paper
- aluminium foil
- coloured crayons
- glue
- silver glitter or crayons (optional)
- black marking pen

Indications:

Skills, techniques, technologies and processes

- Controls a crayon to draw a regular spiral pattern.
- Uses collage as a means of enhancing a simple drawing.

Responding, reflecting on and evaluating visual arts

- Enjoys creating and refining a simple pattern.
- Appreciates that drawing onto coloured paper and using familiar objects to make a collage can combine to bring an imagined creature to 'life'.

Inspiration

- Observe the activities of snails on a rainy day. Note the silvery trails left as they travel.
- List other 'silvery' things about rainy days; for example, raindrops, clouds, windowpanes or lightning.
- Look at snail shells. Compare the shells of sea snails to those of land snails.

Instructions

Step 1

Demonstrate what a spiral is. Invite students to attempt to draw a spiral shape for the class. The students can also use lengths of string or wool to form spiral shapes on the ground, or could practise drawing spirals in chalk on the pavement outside. Provide the students with coloured crayons and paper. Let them carefully draw a 'snail shell' spiral on their page.

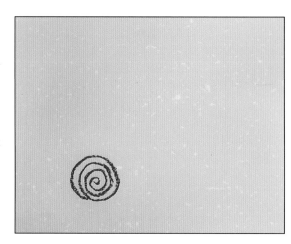

Step 2

Students draw several more snails of different size over their paper. Encourage them to use a variety of different colours to make vibrant, colourful snails. Alternatively, the students may choose to draw either land or sea snails and alter their colouring accordingly. For example, they may choose to use browns only to make land snails.

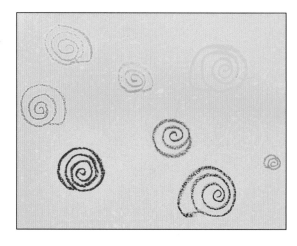

Step 3

Cut or tear strips of aluminium foil. Fold or squash the edges of one piece of foil to make a shape that will fit the available space for a 'trail' behind one of the snail shells. Glue the section of foil behind the snail shell. Repeat this process for the remaining snail shells on the page. The snail trails can be further enhanced with silver glitter or patterns drawn in silver crayons. Use a black marking pen to add the snails' heads and features.

Snail doodles

Step 4 Colour the snails and add a spiral background. Display on black mounting card.

Reflection questions

- Were you able to draw spirals? Was it easy?
- How did you turn your spirals into snails?
- What other things could you draw using spirals?
- How did you make your snail trails?
- How else could you have made snail trails? What other media or materials could you have used?
- What do you think would make the best snail trails? Why?

Variations

- Make snail trails with glitter glue or sand over PVA glue, or strips of smooth plastic, such as cling wrap.
- Use sponges dipped in glittery paint to slide across the page and make snail trails.
- Make other trails by printing the 'feet' shapes of different animals using craft sticks, brushes or other imaginative printing implements.
- Make footprint trails along a long sheet of paper. Use different coloured paints and mix the colours as you walk.

Cross-curricular activities

- Investigate why snails need shells. Find out about other creatures with shells.
- Categorize creatures according to their skeleton type. That is, internal skeletons, external skeletons or shells.
- Students design and label their own ideal home inside a shell shape.
- Observe and feed grass to snails kept in an ice-cream container for an hour.
- Hold snail races and use ordinal numbers to describe the winning sequence.

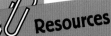

Resources
- light blue card for mounting
- ruler
- coloured pencils
- white paper

Indications:

Skills, techniques, technologies and processes

- Holds a ruler steady as a guide for drawing a straight line.
- Understands what is meant by the term 'random'.

Responding, reflecting on and evaluating visual arts

- Assesses the random lines drawn and notes the closed shapes created by them.
- Reflects upon and attempts to justify the way in which they coloured their drawing.

Inspiration

- Allow students to experiment with drawing straight lines with and without a ruler and compare their results.
- Investigate the uses of rulers.
- Use a ruler to identify edges and lines around the room that are perfectly straight.
- Encourage the students to rule off under their completed work or to underline headings.

Instructions

Step 1

Demonstrate how to rule a line using a ruler. That is, show that one hand is needed to hold the ruler and paper firmly while the other draws the line carefully by sliding the pencil along the edge of the ruler. Give the students time to practise using a ruler if they have not done so before. Allow students to draw a line onto their art paper for the teacher to view. If necessary, assist students individually to help them use a ruler successfully.

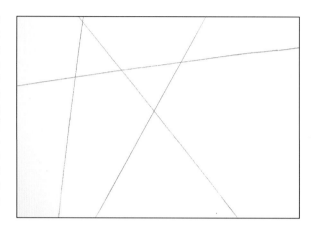

Step 2

Students draw several lines in each colour using coloured pencil. Encourage the students to cover all sections of the page and to vary the angles of the lines they draw to create interesting shapes. Discuss the shapes they have created. Have students identify some of the shapes they find.

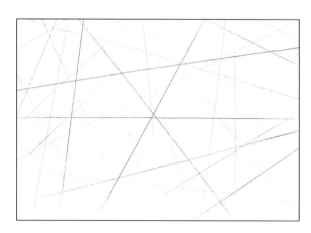

Step 3

Students colour the shapes within their line drawing. The students should not be restricted as to how they go about this. Some will cover several shapes with one colour, while others may choose to colour each shape individually. Discuss the choices made by each student and the reason he/she chose to colour in this way.

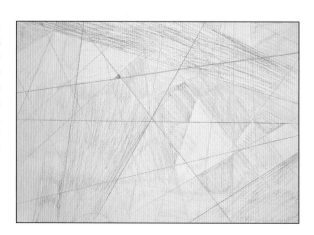

Step 4   If desired, students can enhance their final drawing by selecting several lines to be traced over again and darkened to become dominant. Mount the drawings onto a pastel background to enhance the soft shades achieved using colouring pencils.

Reflection questions

- What did you need to do to make sure each line was ruled straight?
- What types of pictures could you draw using straight lines?
- How did you colour your page? Did you have a system to work out how to colour or did you colour randomly?
- What could you do to make your 'ruler rampage' drawing more interesting?

Variations

- Students rule lines with felt-tipped pens to create their drawing.
- Students rule only one or two lines in each colour.
- Students rule all their lines from a single point on their page (not necessarily in the middle) in one colour, and fill every second 'wedge' with the same colour.
- Students try to write their name using a ruler to form each letter.

Cross-curricular activities

- Encourage students to use a ruler to underline headings or 'rule off' after completed work.
- Use the numbers on a ruler to assist in counting by ones, twos, fives and tens.
- Use a ruler as a 'number line' for use as a concrete aid for adding and subtracting
- Students look at the numbers on a ruler and find patterns; for example, all the 'teens' start with a one.
- Use a ruler to compare lengths; for example, finding things that are longer than, shorter than or about the same length as a ruler.

Resources

- black paint
- fluorescent crayons
- toothpicks
- paintbrush (large flat)
- white paper
- gold card for mounting.
- newspaper

Indications:

Skills, techniques, technologies and processes

- Colours using crayons at an appropriate weight.
- Paints thickly to cover waxy crayons.
- Etches carefully to create shapes and reveal colours.

Responding, reflecting on and evaluating visual arts

- Enjoys the slippery sensation of colouring thickly with crayon.
- Enjoys discovering hidden colours when etching a painted surface.

Inspiration

- Provide faux jewellery, coins and beads to stimulate discussion about valuable jewels and treasure.
- Brainstorm a list of things you might find in a treasure chest.
- Have the students make pasta jewellery and spraypaint in gold or silver. Put the jewellery in a class treasure chest with shiny cellophane 'jewels'.

Instructions

Step 1

Place newspaper onto the students' work surface. This will avoid greasy crayon messes on desks. Use the fluorescent crayons to colour a sheet of white paper completely. Students must press heavily. The colouring can be in patches or wide stripes but need not include any intricate patterning. Explain that this part of the artwork will be painted over and, therefore, any pictures they draw will not be seen.

Step 2

Ensure the students are dressed appropriately in painting shirts. Using black paint at full strength, cover the crayon drawing completely. Encourage the students to cover their crayon drawings thickly, using a wide flat paintbrush. Allow the paint to dry completely.

Step 3

Brainstorm the types of things that might be found in a treasure chest. Encourage the students to demonstrate how to draw some of these items for other students. Demonstrate how the crayon colours are revealed when the paint is scratched away. Provide the students with toothpicks to use to scratch away drawings of the things they might find in their treasure chest.

Discovering treasur

Step 4   Make a frame from gold card to place over the 'treasure chest'. Turn to the reverse, holding firmly, and attach with sticky tape. Alternatively, display the artworks adjacent to each other and cut a large dome 'lid' and a border from gold card to create a treasure chest to frame all of the students' work.

Reflection questions

- How did you make your jewels and treasure look precious?
- Was it easy to scratch away the paint layer? What might have made it easier?
- What colours stand out best against black?
- How else could you have framed your artwork to make it more like a treasure chest?

Variations

- Scratch away large areas of paint to draw pictures such as colourful balloons or flowers.
- Scratch away radiating patterns to create fireworks in a night sky.
- Use an alternative paint colour to create a different environment; for example, green for a garden or blue for a day sky.

Cross-curricular activities

- Allow the students to dress up in pretend jewellery to act out stories about jewel robberies or pirates.
- Allow the students to pretend they are buying and selling at a shop. Provide play money.
- Investigate coins, noting their values, sizes and pictures.
- Solve simple money problems.

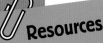

Resources

- white paper
- coloured crayons
- red card for mounting
- circle template (block or lid etc.)
- scissors

Indications:

Skills, techniques, technologies and processes

- Tracks the direction of lines to create concentric and parallel lines.
- Repeats regular, repetitive patterns

Responding, reflecting on and evaluating visual arts

- Reflects upon the colours chosen and how they contribute to the overall visual appeal of the artwork.
- Appreciates that regular patterns can be used to create fabrics, papers and other materials or simply to create art.

Inspiration

- Find regular patterns used in advertising brochures and fabrics.
- Look through a kaleidoscope to see how the lines, shapes and colours interchange.
- Identify patterns occurring in nature. Some good examples include spider webs, snake skins, and patterning on animals' fur, such as on leopards, giraffes and zebras.

Instructions

Step 1

Show the students examples of fabrics where patterns have been used. Explain that they will be creating their own design for a fabric pattern using parallel and concentric lines. Demonstrate what is meant by 'concentric' and 'parallel'. Invite students to draw lines parallel to a line drawn. Repeat the process for concentric lines, having the students draw lines inside a circle you have traced. Allow students to use a template to draw several circles in crayon on a large sheet of white paper.

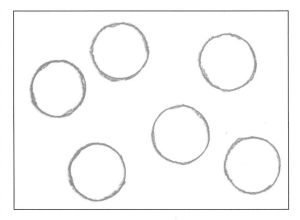

Step 2

Students draw concentric lines within the circles they have traced. Alternate colours with each line drawn and consider the thickness of the lines. The design will look best if all lines are a similar thickness. This is not a rule, of course, and the students should be encouraged to be as creative with their design as they like.

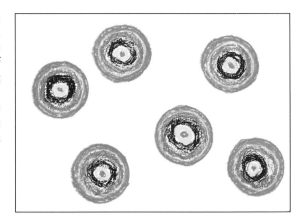

Step 3

Allow the students to draw straight lines between each of the circles and between the circles and the edge of the page. The students can then draw parallel lines on either side of each of those lines, using one colour at a time for each line, until the gaps close and no white paper remains.

Fabric design

Step 4 Mount the fabric design pattern against a bright red background. Alternatively, have the students draw an item of clothing onto the red mounting card. The drawing should be big enough to frame a large portion of the artwork. They can then cut away the internal shape they drew to create a frame. The students will require help to cut out their internal shape. Place the completed frame over the fabric design artwork and cut away any excess drawing at the edges. Attach with sticky tape to secure.

Reflection questions

- Do you think parallel lines and concentric circles look good together?
- How else could you have combined these two types of line to create a pattern?
- How would you describe the colours you chose to use? Bright? Pastel? Warm? Cool?
- Do you think your pattern would look good as a fabric design?
- What type of fabric would your design suit best? Heavy? Silky? Woolly?

Variations

- Build parallel lines around other shapes.
- Continue concentric lines around circles until they merge together.
- Use tight zigzags to create thick lines for making patterns.
- Design a garment and draw a pattern in its shape to enhance the garment.
- Paint patterns onto calico and make simple garments from it, such as Christmas stockings, cushion covers or library bags.

Cross-curricular activities

- Investigate what clothing is made from. What natural materials are needed to produce the clothing materials?
- Find out about the national costumes of other countries.
- Debate whether or not we **need** to wear clothes.
- Hold days where the students are required to 'dress up' as something special to them.

Resources
- brightly coloured card for mounting
- coloured crayons
- white paper

Indications:

Skills, techniques, technologies and processes

- Uses imagination to create something unique or unexpected.
- Uses a drawing medium to represent ideas.

Responding, reflecting on and evaluating visual arts

- Assesses the impact of their imaginative choices through the responses of others to their drawing.
- Imagines their creature in the flesh and compares the image they drew to what they visualised.

Inspiration

- Brainstorm different kinds of body coverings and animal body parts. Students imagine other kinds of body coverings and body parts and add them to the list.
- As a whole class, draw an imaginary creature using body parts from the list to create the most unusual creature possible.

Instructions

Step 1

Students imagine they have their own head on a different body. Encourage the students to share what body they would choose and why. What environment would they live in? How would they move? Explain that they are to create a creature with a head and body not usually seen together; for example, a bird's head with a fish body. Encourage the students to come up with the craziest and most unusual combination they can. Ask them to point to where the middle of the page is. Ask them to draw the head of their creature so that it fits above the imaginary line across the middle of their page. Students think about how the head and body will fit together and how to allow for that in their drawing.

Step 2

Students draw the body of their creature using the bottom section of the page, so that it joins to the head. The students should be encouraged to use up as much of the page as they can.

Step 3

Students add any detail that will make their creature more individual. Suggest that the creature may need something added to it to help it move or survive in its new environment.

Imaginative drawing

Step 4

Students draw and colour a background to represent the new environment for the imaginative creature. Use brightly coloured card to mount the creature and accentuate the 'crazy' nature of the subject.

Reflection questions

- Have you ever seen a creature like the one you drew?
- What features are your favourites? Why do you like these the best?
- Do you think your drawing is interesting to other people who look at it? What makes it interesting?
- Was it fun thinking up something new?
- How did you draw your background? What is the creature's environment meant to be? Why did you think this type of environment would be most suitable for your creature?

Variations

- Use imagination to draw other 'new' ideas; for example, an imaginary plant, flower, building, space creature, insect or food
- Students draw a particular creature and cut their creatures in half (at the 'waist'). Make a display of mismatched imaginary creatures.
- Students draw their pet with something added that is 'not quite normal'.

Cross-curricular activities

- Students write short stories telling what their life might be like as someone else or as an animal or bird.
- Read stories about imagination such as 'Where the wild things are' by Maurice Sendak.
- Discuss the difference between what is real and what is make-believe. Use television shows or movies to illustrate.
- Students imagine they are shopkeepers, parents, teachers, doctors or vets in a role-playing corner or when acting out short stories.

Resources

- green and blue crayons
- scissors
- water
- blue paint
- paintbrush (wide, flat)
- blue and black card for mounting
- white paper
- black fine-tipped pen
- lead pencil

Indications:

Skills, techniques, technologies and processes

- Draws lines to represent pondweed.
- Spaces pondweed and tadpoles to create a balanced picture.

Responding, reflecting on and evaluating visual arts

- Understands that using certain media can create a watery impression.
- Appreciates that the way a picture is mounted can enhance the image.

Inspiration

- Keep frog eggs in a fishbowl and observe how the frogs develop and grow.
- Discuss what might be kept in a fish tank or have students who own fish tanks describe theirs to the class.
- Discuss the different shapes of known and imaginary fish tanks.

Instructions

Step 1

Provide students with a selection of green crayons. Discuss the variety available. Students attempt to describe the different types of green. Allow the students to draw a series of squiggly lines vertically on their page in each green-coloured crayon. Encourage the students to spread out the colours and to try to make their lines look as if they are floating underwater like pondweed would.

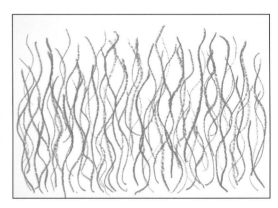

Step 2

Show the students a black felt-tipped pen. Discuss how a felt-tipped pen should be used, and the type of use that would damage such a pen. Students demonstrate careful use of these 'special' pens for their peers. Discuss what tadpoles look like at various stages of development. Students decide how old their tadpoles are going to be and then carefully draw them among their squiggly 'pondweed' lines using a black felt-tipped pen.

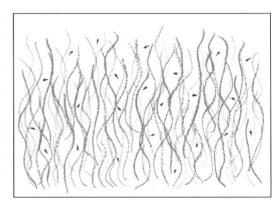

Step 3

Ensure the students have newspaper spread across their work area and are appropriately attired in art shirts ready to paint. Prepare a medium strength solution of blue paint and water (one part paint to two parts water). Students use a wide, flat brush to paint their drawings completely. Explain that it is not necessary for the blue colour to be uniform and that variations in the brightness of the paint will make their painting look more 'watery'. Blurring of the tadpoles when exposed to water will produce a similar illusion.

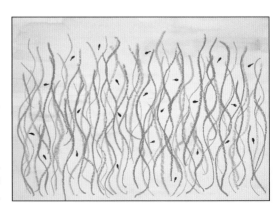

Tadpole pond

Step 4   Allow the students to 'invent' a fishbowl shape and draw it onto mounting card. They can then cut away the internal shape they drew to create a fish bowl frame for their drawing. The students will require help to cut out their internal shape. Place the completed frame over the tadpole drawing and cut away any excess drawing at the edges. Attach with sticky tape and mount on a black background.

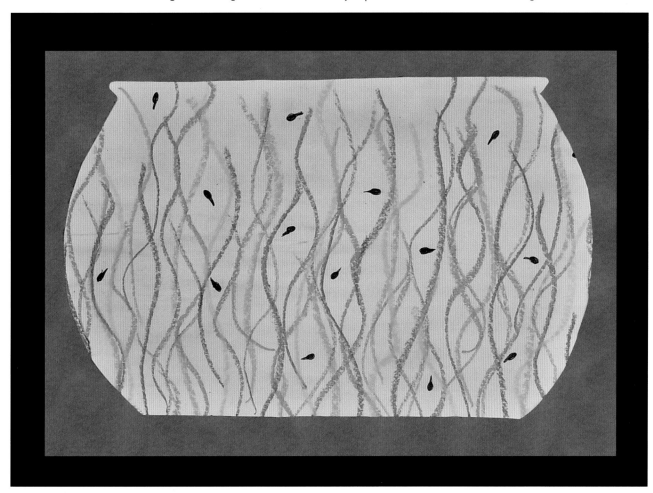

Reflection questions

- How did you give the impression your tadpoles were in a watery environment?
- Do you think the environment in your watery picture would be a place tadpoles could be happy? Why?
- What happened when you painted over the crayon pondweed?
- What do you think might have happened if you had drawn the tadpoles while the paint was still wet?

Cross-curricular activities

- Track the development of a tadpole into a frog. Investigate simple life cycles.
- Discuss growing up. Have the students identify things they can do now that they couldn't do when they were babies.
- Measure the students' heights on a height chart.
- Students order themselves from shortest to tallest.
- Write personal goals for something they want to do when they grow bigger.

Variations

- Students use a paint wash over other crayon pictures to make them stand out or to create a background.
- Students use felt-tip pens to draw circles close together with tiny tadpoles curled inside them to look like frog eggs. Wash over in a bright 'caviar' colour and watch the pen blur to create a watery effect.
- Students make borders of other fishbowls or tank shapes.

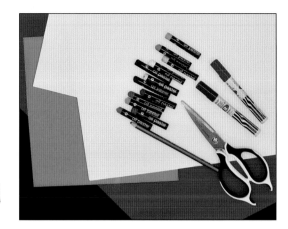

Resources

- two sheets white paper
- lead pencil
- scissors
- crayons
- thick red and blue markers
- black, red and blue card for mounting
- two pieces of music, one slow and quiet and one fast and loud

Indications:

Skills, techniques, technologies and processes

- Chooses colours appropriate to a situation or mood.
- Listens to music and responds artistically with a chosen drawing medium.

Responding, reflecting on and evaluating visual arts

- Understands that art and music are means of expression.
- Responds to music with colour and line variations to create a visual 'mood'.

Inspiration

- Listen to different types of music. Students describe how the music makes them feel. Note the colours the music reminds them of.
- Students make high and low, fast and slow and staccato or smooth noises.
- Students describe other types of noise in terms of colour.

Instructions

Step 1

The students will require adult assistance to prepare the musical note on which to mount the response to the music. Ideally, a large musical note can be drawn onto black card and cut out by the students. If black card is unavailable, the students can paint sheets of paper black, wait until dry and repeat the process on the reverse side. Musical notes can then be drawn and cut out accordingly.

Prepare two pieces of paper of identical oval shape for the students to draw their responses on. These shapes will need to be slightly smaller than the oval shape of the black musical note made previously.

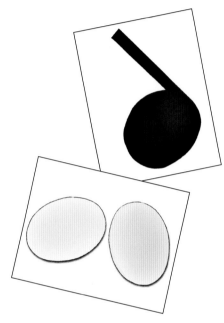

Step 2

Play a piece of music that is slow and quiet. Ask the students to describe the music. Allow them to dance quietly and slowly to the music. Write the words 'slow and quiet' for the students to see and ask the students to write these words along the bottom of one of their oval shapes. Alternatively, an adult could write these for the students. Ask the students what kinds of colours could represent quiet, slow music. Ensure the students have access to crayons in these colours. Play the piece of music again and allow the students to draw lines and shapes which 'look and feel' quiet and slow.

Step 3

Play a piece of loud, fast music for the students to hear and dance to. Ask the students to think about how it makes them feel, the colours they think of and the images they see. Students (or an adult) write the words 'fast and loud' along the bottom of the second oval shape. Allow the students to draw a response as the loud, fast music is played again.

Musical patterns

Step 4

Attach the ovals to either side of the musical note. The note can then be suspended from the ceiling. Alternatively, they may be displayed side by side along a wall. Thread a length of fishing line through the outer edge of the oval shape of each black musical note. This will enable the notes to be flipped in unison from side to side. The notes can then be used as an indicator of the type of activity the students will be participating in. For example, independent reading time could be represented by the 'quiet' side, or tidying up could be represented by the 'fast' side.

Reflection questions

- What kinds of lines and colours did you use to describe quiet noises?
- What kinds of lines and colours did you use to describe loud noises?
- How did you feel as you drew to the music? Did it change the way you felt like drawing?

Variations

- Students listen to stimulating music as they complete other creative or artistic tasks.
- Students consider the colours they use to complete scary pictures or sad pictures.
- Make advertisements using eye-catching 'loud' colours and patterns.

Cross-curricular activities

- Students move or dance to different types of music to describe it.
- Discuss feelings and situations that might make you feel scared, sleepy, excited, glad or surprised.
- Learn simple songs and use instruments to accompany them.
- Use percussion instruments to simulate everyday noises such as running, wind or rain.

Indications:

Skills, techniques, technologies and processes

- Manipulates a variety of drawing media to create variations in weight and style.
- Creates depth and atmosphere by 'layering' in different styles and weights of lines.

Responding, reflecting on and evaluating visual arts

- Assesses the 'balance' of the final drawing by identifying areas which are 'heavy' or overdone.
- Describes how adding small amounts of bright colours changes his/her drawing.

Inspiration

- Take the students for a 'nature walk' to note different types of leaves and bark and their textures.
- Have the students make rubbings of 'natural' items such as leaves, rocks and bark and compare their patterns.
- View *Surprised!* by Rousseau (1891), the first of his jungle scenes, which contain dense vegetation.

Resources

- green card for mounting
- green, yellow, blue and brown crayons or pencils
- 1 purple, 1 red and 1 orange fluorescent crayon
- blue and yellow crayons or pencils
- white paper

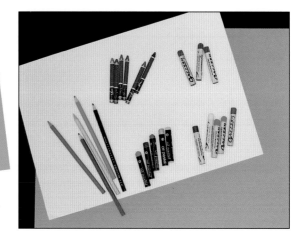

Instructions

Step 1

Provide the students with a variety of green and brown crayons. Explain that they will be creating a garden full of different types of textures. Recall some of the textures the students have seen in gardens before. Group the plants they have seen into smooth, rounded plants and rough, jagged plants. Ask the students to use the green and brown crayons to draw the rough and jagged things they might find in their garden. Encourage the students to fill the page right to the top corners so that when they are finished their garden will look like what a beetle would see if it was standing in it.

Step 2

Provide the students with blue and yellow crayons. Ask the students to draw all of the smooth, rounded things they might find in their garden. Again, encourage the students to fill the page, closing any gaps from their first drawings to create a thickly vegetated garden.

Step 3

Provide the students with bright fluorescent crayons in orange, red and purple. These colours should contrast with the other colours used. Ask the students to draw flowers or insects using these bright colours to bring their garden to life.

Texture garden

Step 4 Students' work can be mounted individually, or massed together so that they overlap, or be attached to a display wall at an angle. The students can then glue on crepe paper streamers, brightly coloured tissue paper and other textured materials to complete the textured garden display. The display could be further enhanced by adding words written in interesting fonts which describe the textures in the display.

Reflection questions
- Did you fill your page?
- How would you describe the green and brown plants you drew?
- How are your blue and yellow plant lines different from your green and brown lines?
- Does your picture look like a garden? What kind of garden?
- Does your garden look better or worse with the flowers? Why?

Variations
- Make a spooky garden drawing in dark colours only. Add 'spooky' night creatures, camouflaged but with bright eyes.
- Draw a garden full of yellow flowers and one purple flower in contrast. Talk about why the purple flower 'draws the eye' to it.
- Draw a leafy green house plant with a brightly coloured beetle on it.

Cross-curricular activities
- Compare and sort different types of leaves into categories.
- Grow plants in a class garden.
- Investigate things that grow in gardens.
- Identify what living things need to live and grow.
- Compare the needs of plants to the needs of people or animals.
- Explore the senses using leaves – how they smell, feel and look.
- Taste a variety of raw and cooked vegetables.

Resources

- lead pencil
- black crayon
- metallic crayons
- coloured pencils
- greasy crayons
- scissors
- white paper
- brown, orange and grey paper squares
- glue
- maroon card for mounting
- blocks (optional)

Indications:

Skills, techniques, technologies and processes

- Draws simple closed shapes to create imagined building blocks for a medieval castle.
- Uses a variety of drawing media to colour closed shapes.

Responding, reflecting on and evaluating visual arts

- Understands that colour and shape combine to create an atmosphere in a drawing.
- Appreciates that different media suit different drawing styles.

Inspiration

- Introduce closed and open shapes. Look at how closed shapes can be used to depict 3-D objects.
- Students build towers out of blocks. The students can then attempt to draw their 3-D castle in a 2-D drawing.
- Look at and discuss castles. Note the dark colours and how they make the castle appear old and worn.

Instructions

Step 1

Brainstorm to name and list a variety of shapes. Allow the students to build towers with building blocks to familiarise themselves with the way blocks can fit together and support one another. Students draw a castle which includes blocks of all shapes and sizes and is as tall as the page.

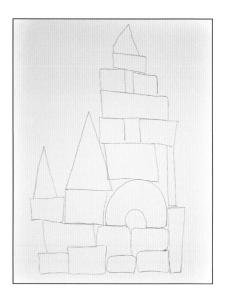

Step 2

Students select all the colours a spooky castle might be; for example, browns, greys, maroons and oranges. The crayons can be a combination of greasy crayons, waxy crayons and metallic crayons. The students can use these colours to colour the blocks in their castle. Encourage the students to use their colours randomly across the blocks instead of having all the brown blocks together in one area. However, if a student can justify that he or she is following a predetermined system of colouring, he/she should be encouraged to colour following the chosen system.

Step 3

Glue grey, orange and brown paper scraps on a large sheet of paper. This will become the background for the castle.

2-D shape castle

Step 4

Outline the block shapes in black crayon and cut around the exterior of the castle. Glue the castle onto the background to give a semi-camouflaged, 'dark' effect for their spooky castle. If desired, the students might like to cut out bat shapes from black paper and glue them on their castle pictures. Mount the castle picture on a maroon background.

Reflection questions

- What kind of atmosphere did you create with the colours you chose?
- How old do you think your castle might be?
- How is your picture a castle, as distinct from other types of buildings? How did you achieve this look?
- What could you add to your drawing to make it appear spookier?

Variations

- Encourage students to break down other things they attempt to draw into the shapes they see.
- Draw other types of buildings in the same way. Students consider the colours they choose to reflect the age and materials used in the building.
- Attempt to draw simple 3-D shapes to create a building.

Cross-curricular activities

- Students imagine and write creepy stories about living or staying in an old castle.
- Challenge the students to build a tower to a certain height, given set materials.
- Investigate how things have changed over time. In particular, discuss similarities and differences in lifestyle, including changes in food, clothing and shelter.

Resources
- coloured pencils
- scissors
- lead pencil
- white paper
- gold card for mounting
- sticky tape

Indications:

Skills, techniques, technologies and processes:

- Represents self through drawing.
- Understands the position and general proportions of facial features.

Responding, reflecting on and evaluating visual arts

- Accepts approximations of facial features in own drawing of self.
- Appreciates that portraits can be used as a means of documenting history.

Inspiration

- Look at self-portraits by artists such as Matisse and Rembrandt.
- Introduce the term 'portrait' and deduce what is meant by a 'self-portrait'.
- Students look in a mirror and note their defining facial features and how they are alike and different from their peers.

Instructions

Step 1

Students explore their own faces by touch. Encourage them to identify where features start and finish in relation to other features. For example, their eyes are in the middle of their head (not at the top) and their ears line up between their eyebrows and the bottom of their nose and are long rather than round. Discuss the shape of their face. Is it long? Round? Square? Allow the students to use a lead pencil to draw their face shape and then add the eyes, nose, mouth and ears to demonstrate their proportion.

Step 2

Students identify additional features on their face as well as their hair type and style. The students can then add these distinguishing details to their drawings to make their self-portraits more personal.

Step 3

Cut two rectangular strips of gold card long enough to frame the drawing. One strip may need to be longer than the other. (One for length, the other for width). Cut the strips lengthways using a wavy or zigzag line to create the sides of a portrait frame. Alternatively, use craft scissors to create a more intricately-patterned border.

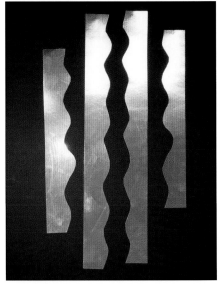

Portrait drawing

Step 4

Colour the final portrait using coloured pencils. Join the ends of the gold cardboard frame to form a rectangular or square frame. Use glue sparingly on the back of the frame and carefully place it over the self-portrait in a position that best enhances the picture. When the frame has dried, trim away any excess paper from the original portrait drawing.

Reflection questions

- Does your self-portrait look like you? What is the same? What is different?
- What kinds of lines did you use to describe different parts of your face?
- What could you do to make your portrait more realistic? What other media would work better than pencil?

Variations

- Draw portraits of peers.
- Use other media to create a portrait.
- Experiment with drawing profiles.
- Trace the profile of a peers face using a long pencil and butchers' paper.
- Practise drawing close-ups of particular parts of the face; for example, an eye, ear, lips or teeth.

Cross-curricular activities

- Discuss things that make you unique, including special features, skills and qualities.
- Compare a variety of breeds of one type of animal. Review how they are alike and different.
- Students nominate a skill or quality they are good at. They make plans to develop and improve that skill or quality.

Glossary – Drawing

balance	harmony of design, colour and proportion
calico	a rough cotton cloth, usually off-white in colour
closed shape	shape with complete boundary
concentric	having the same centre; for example, when a stone is dropped into water, the ripples form concentric circles
dominant	ruling, prevailing, or most influential element
etch	to cut or eat into a surface; for example, acid eating into metal
faux	not real, a false substitute
kaleidoscope	a tube with mirrors and pieces of coloured glass in one end which shows different patterns when it is turned around
layering	the process of applying a medium or media in layers so that all layers are partially exposed
medium	a means or material used by an artist to produce a work of art
open shape	shape without a completed boundary, a line
parallel	lines which are the same distance from each other at every point
percussion	musical instruments used to produce a beat or note when they are struck
portrait	(a) a painting, drawing or photograph of someone, especially of their face; (b) rectangular paper placed vertically (as against landscape)
profile	an outline drawing of a face, especially a side view
radiating pattern	a pattern that spreads out like rays from a centre
random	happening or being done without a plan or purpose
rubbings	reproduced patterns or designs created by rubbing paper laid over a surface with a soft medium, such as chalk
self-portrait	portrait made by a person of himself or herself
shade	to create a darker or lighter version of one colour
staccato	an instruction in music to make notes sharply separate
template	a precut cardboard design used as a guide for drawing or cutting out a closed shape
Venn diagram	set of circles representing logical classes which may or may not coincide or intersect

Useful websites

Artists and movements

Henri Matisse Art Gallery	www.geocities.com/Paris/LeftBank/4208/
WebMuseum: Rembrandt Van Rijn	www.ibiblio.org/wm/paint/auth/rembrandt/
The Museum of Modern Art	www.moma.org
Terminology and art index	www.artlex.com
Art Museum network	www.amn.org

Tools and techniques

Figure drawings and portraits	www.figuredrawings.com/drawingsofpeople.html

Art education

Composition and design	www.goshen.edu/art/ed/Compose.htm
The incredible art department	www.princetonol.com/groups/iad/
Magical places and creative spaces	www.allthedaze.com

PAINTING

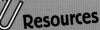

Resources
- paints in primary and secondary colours
- scissors
- paintbrush
- white art paper
- yellow card for mounting
- newspaper

Indications:

Skills, techniques, technologies and processes

- Controls a paintbrush in order to copy a given shape or pattern.
- Paints within a boundary.
- Cuts carefully around the exterior boundary of a shape.

Responding, reflecting on and evaluating visual arts

- Enjoys the challenge of reproducing the artwork of another person.
- Identifies similarities and differences between their own and other artworks.

Inspiration

- Look at pictures with clean lines in sharply contrasting colours.
- Expose the students to pictures of modern art where strong colours are well defined.
- Conduct activities where the students are given the opportunity to listen and follow instructions; for example, blindfolded walks and 'Simon says'-style games.

Instructions

Step 1

For this activity, the students are required to follow step-by-step modelling or verbal instructions provided by the teacher, an assistant or a peer. Creativity will be limited to the students' interpretation of verbal commands and visual stimuli modelled for them. All of the students' approximations for copying a modelled painting should be accepted and praised.

Ensure the student has been provided with newspaper or other protective covering for his/her work surface. Demonstrate how to 'load' a paint brush so that it holds adequate paint without dripping.

Model or describe a red circle for the students to replicate in the middle of their own page.

When the students have painted their circles, demonstrate returning the paint brush to its matching paint colour so as not to mix colours.

Step 2

Repeat the modelling process one step at a time, allowing each student to complete the given direction before proceeding to the next.

Emphasise the importance of keeping colours unmixed and vibrant through careful use of the paintbrush. Use the dragon picture shown or create your own mythical creature for the students to copy.

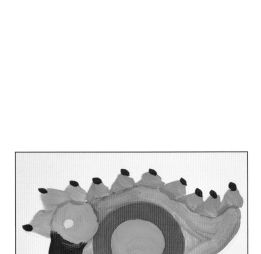

Step 3

Use scissors to cut around the painted shape. Leave a border of white paper no more than one centimetre around the shape. This will help the painting stand out against the background chosen as a mount. Discard the paper cut away.

Directed painting

Step 4   Mount the mythical creature on coloured card. Choose a colour that will give a strong contrast to the colours used in the painting. The students should be encouraged to make this choice based on their own opinion of what 'looks good'.

Reflection questions
- Are my colours bold and unmixed?
- Did I follow instructions well?
- Is my painting bright and clear?
- Did I keep myself and my equipment tidy?
- Did I use the colours I was asked to use?
- Am I happy with the finished product?
- Did I enjoy making my painting?

Variations
- Brainstorm to list and discuss mythical creatures such as elves, fairies and unicorns as an alternative, 'open-ended' subject to a dragon.
- Students describe a painting for their peers to copy.
- Paint on brightly coloured paper.
- Provide easels for painting and allow the students to draw their own creative version of an imaginary subject.

Cross-curricular activities
- Play colour games to consolidate colour recognition.
- Play listening or 'barrier' games to give students practice for directed painting.
- Play 'blind' games where the students take turns to verbally direct their peers.
- Encourage visual discrimination by having students identify changes in a picture or group of objects.
- Focus on the senses—particularly sight—as a means of appreciating visual arts.

Resources

- yellow, brown, white, orange and black paint in squirt bottles
- black marking pen
- pencil
- green card for mounting
- newspaper
- white paper
- scissors
- glue

Indications:

Skills, techniques, technologies and processes

- Attempts to create an impression of familiar textures.
- Uses fingers as a tool for creating patterns and directing paint.

Responding, reflecting on and evaluating visual arts

- Enjoys using fingers to slide through textured paint and create patterns.
- Imagines and attempts to create patterns to depict different types of hair.

Inspiration

- Students explore different textures, including playdough, wet sand and other materials, which are viscous or 'slide' between the fingers.
- Allow the students to fingerpaint using a detergent-based paint on plastic sheeting or glass to experiment with different patterns, lines and prints.

Instructions

Step 1

Draw an outline of a hairless dog. The outline will need to be large enough to be fingerpainted and be positioned towards the bottom of the page to allow room for 'hair' to be added. The students may require adult assistance to complete this task. Alternatively, the teacher can pre-prepare the outlines by drawing one in thick marking pen and copying onto light card or heavy art paper.

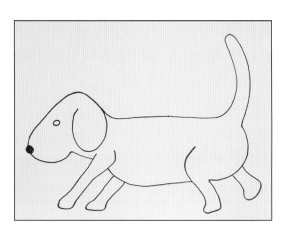

Step 2

Squirt blobs of paint across the top of the dog's body. Encourage the students to think about what hair colours dogs have and to squirt on a combination of these colours.

Step 3

Use fingers to spread the paint across the dog's body to create fur. Discuss the different types of fur dogs can have: curly, straight, spiky, tufty. Make swirling, curvy or straight linear patterns to represent the texture of the fur along the dog's back. The students may also like to experiment with their fingernails or knuckles to create interesting patterns.

Hairy dogs

Step 4   Cut out a 'fur' outline around the painted dog. This outline may follow the boundary of the painted area or be cut into the paint in a design that will enhance a curly or spiky painting. Add detail to the face or body if desired and mount on a green background.

Reflection questions

- How did the paint feel in your fingers?
- What kinds of patterns and prints can you make with your fingers?
- Did the pattern you chose to make with your fingers suit your animal?
- What else would finger-painting patterns be good for making?
- Did you cut out a good animal shape?

Variations

- Fingerpaint onto a plastic or glass surface and take a paper print of the pattern or picture you created.
- Fingerpaint patterns to make hair on a self-portrait.
- Use fingerpainting to create a background for a collage.
- Use fingerpainting as a means of exploring new colours; combine to make new colours.

Cross-curricular activities

- Use the animal paintings to classify dogs into groups according to their fur type; for example, straight, curly or wavy.
- Investigate a variety of dogs and what makes them alike and different.
- Investigate opposites and words used to describe textures: for example, sharp – smooth, curly – straight.

Indications:

Skills, techniques, technologies and processes

- Experiments with textured paint.
- Uses tools other than paintbrushes to spread textured paint.

Responding, reflecting on and evaluating visual arts

- Appreciates the unique effect produced when using soap paint.
- Chooses appropriate tools for working with a unique medium.

Inspiration

- Allow the students to 'play' and become familiar with soap paint, using their hands to spread and pile it up on a plastic surface.
- Select students to participate in mixing the soap flakes into their frothy form ready for soap painting. Discuss how air becomes trapped inside the tiny bubbles of the soap paint to make it light and frothy.
- Discuss subjects that would suit being painted out of soap; for example, things that need washing or other items where bubbles might be found.

Instructions

Step 1

Draw an outline of a pig onto grey or silver card. The outline will need to be large enough to be painted using frothy soap paint with simple boundaries for the soap to be spread to. The students may require adult assistance to complete this task. Alternatively, pre-prepare the outlines by drawing one in thick marking pen and copying onto light card or heavy art paper.

Step 2

Place half a cup of cold water in a large mixing bowl. Beat on high speed while slowly adding one cup of soap flakes. The mixture will froth and expand as it is mixed. Add pink paint and mix for a further 10 seconds. Repeat this process until enough soap paint has been produced for the number of students in the group. One cup of beaten soap flakes will be sufficient for two students.

Step 3

Provide the students with tools suitable for spreading the soapy medium. Move the 'paint' around the page to meet the boundaries of the piggy shape. Aim to have a fairly consistent thickness of paint covering all areas of the pig. Add glitter if desired. Allow the painting to dry over several days. The paintings will be fragile when dry so should not be handled too much at this final stage.

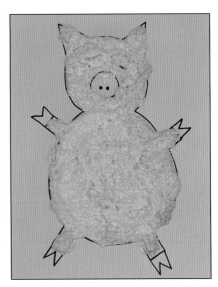

Soapy piggy

Step 4

Draw a bathtub shape around the piggy on grey or silver card. Highlight the bathtub shape by framing in foil. Cut out the piggy in the bathtub and mount on a pink background to display.

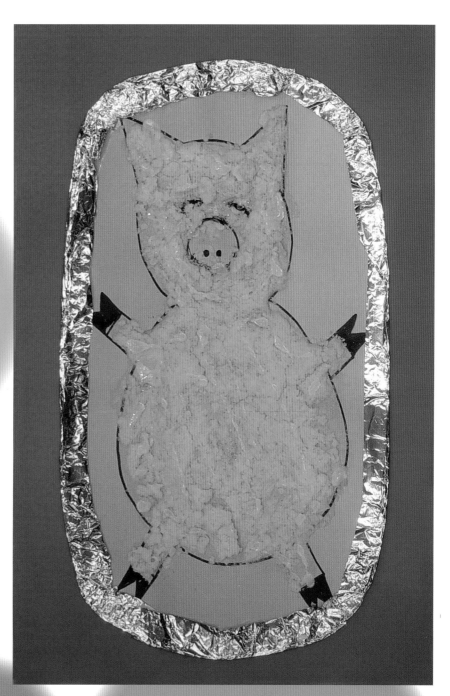

Reflection questions

- What was the subject of your soap painting? Why do you think this subject suited a painting made of soap?
- How did you spread the soap paint over the page? What tools did you use?
- How would you describe soap paint? Was it fun to use?

Variations

- Allow the students to fingerpaint with soap paint to create their own free patterns and pictures.
- Put soap paint onto aluminium foil and add glitter while the soap flakes are wet.
- Use icing bags to 'pipe' soap paint in different colours on to a page to create a picture.

Cross-curricular activities

- Review personal hygiene habits. Encourage the students to wash their hands before eating.
- Investigate animals that like mud.
- Write short stories about a naughty little piggy who is always getting dirty.
- Visit a farmyard or invite a baby animal farm to the school for the students to view and experience.
- Discuss why it is important to keep clean.
- Share experiences the students have had visiting the doctor when they have been sick.

Indications:

Skills, techniques, technologies and processes

- Uses squirt bottles to apply paint on a page.
- Uses gravity to move paint around the page and creates a pleasing effect.

Responding, reflecting on and evaluating visual arts

- Assesses how much mixing is 'enough' before producing a 'messy' result.
- Evaluates the appropriateness of salt paint for the task given.

Inspiration

- Look at the night sky or pictures of it.
- Look through a kaleidoscope and watch large shapes break into small shapes.
- Look at space pictures of vibrant celestial activity such as a supernova. Note the brilliance of colour and the iridescent effect.

Instructions

Step 1

Use a wide brush to paint a piece of art paper black. Set aside and allow to dry completely. The painted paper will create a stiff surface on which to use the salt paint.

Step 2

Make salt paints by mixing equal parts of paint and salt. Salt will make some paint colours quite runny initially and may require additional salt to be added in order to create a thicker consistency suitable for squirting from squeeze bottles.

Squirt paint in blobs all over the page. Use colours both side by side and one on top of another, creating a layered effect.

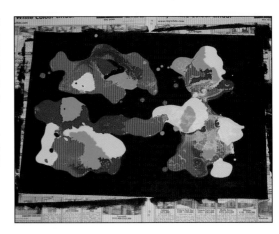

Step 3

Hold the paper up and tilt the page, causing the paints to run into one another to develop a 'cosmic' effect. Stop tilting after short intervals and reassess the artwork. If the colours are overworked they will become too mixed and lose their effect. The students should be encouraged to think about when to stop rather than changing and adding to their work. However, in some cases, it may be necessary to reapply some colours in very small amounts if they are lost in the tilting process. Set the artwork aside on a completely flat surface to dry.

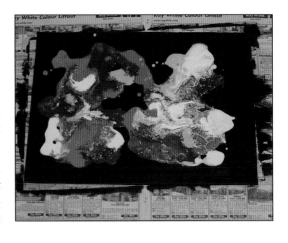

Cosmic lights

Step 4 When completely dry, the salt will give the paint a sparkly, glittery effect. To enhance the 'sparkles', use gold or silver card for mounting. Alternatively, hang all the students work side by side to create a 'cosmic universe' display. The students may also wish to add foil stars or glitter to the black areas.

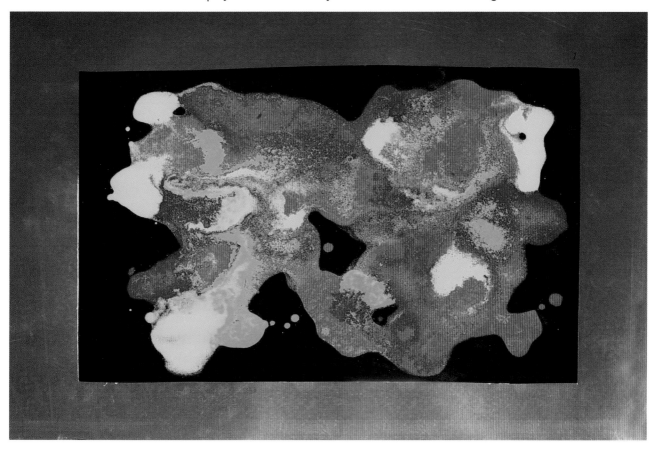

Reflection questions

- Did your painting turn out as you anticipated?
- Was it difficult or easy to use salt paint? How was it different?
- Did you mix your paint on the page enough? Too much?
- Would you do anything different next time?
- Does your picture look like something from outer space?

Variations

- Try using a thicker or thinner version of the salt paint by adding more or less salt and compare the results.
- Try using an eye-dropper or straw to collect and deposit smaller quantities of paint. The aim is to create a spotted or speckled appearance rather than mixing the colours.
- Paint onto brightly coloured or textured card.

Cross-curricular activities

- Explore constellations. Students design their own constellations by putting pin-pricks in black paper and holding them up to the light.
- Investigate things that can shine, such as mirrors, lights or water.
- Compare light and dark. Discuss the things that can happen in each environment.
- Discuss sounds you could hear in the dark. Imagine what sounds cosmic lights might make.
- Make a sound effects tape of night noises.

Resources

- glass
- detergent
- blue and white paint
- paintbrush
- light and dark blue coloured paper
- newspaper
- sponge

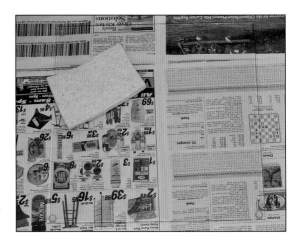

Indications:

Skills, techniques, technologies and processes

- Paints simple pictures onto glass using a wide paint brush.
- Cuts umbrella shapes and fastens them to a glass surface using paint.

Responding, reflecting on and evaluating visual arts

- Attempts to create a 'rainy' atmosphere through painting.
- Appreciates the translucent nature of paint on glass against a bright background.

Inspiration

- Watch rain on the windowpanes on a rainy day.
- Observe and discuss different types of rain.
- Experiment with tap or coloured water on butcher's paper, using different techniques such as splattering, dropping, spraying and so on.
- Watch drops forming and falling into water.

Instructions

Step 1

Choose an area of glass suitable for painting. Windows are ideal as the changing weather will show through, creating a changing background for the rain picture. This will also demonstrate the changing moods that can be achieved as a background is altered.

Use a damp cloth to clean the glass and prepare it for painting.

Mix the paint to be used with a small amount of detergent. This will make cleaning the glass easier when clear glass is required again.

Step 2

Paint raindrops all over the surface. The drops can be blue, white or a combination of both on one paintbrush. They should also be of varying size to give the effect of some being closer while others are further away.

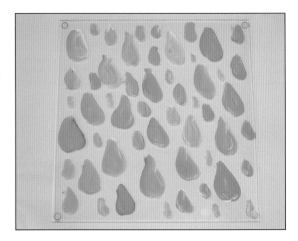

Step 3

Cut out umbrella shapes from light and dark blue coloured paper squares. Attach them randomly to the bottom of the painting, using small amounts of paint. The umbrellas can vary in size or be identical. Alternatively, use brightly coloured paper scraps to make a collage of colourful designs on brightly coloured umbrellas.

Step 4

Using a fine paintbrush, add handles to the umbrellas and tiny white and pale blue water droplets between the large drops. Watch the atmosphere of the painting change as the weather changes from sunny to cloudy and day to night.

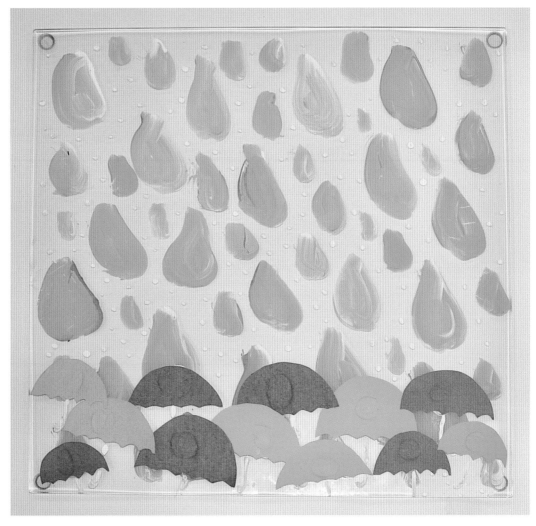

Reflection questions

- Did the water droplets look like real droplets on the glass?
- What kind of sky do your droplets look best against? Cloudy? Sunny?
- What did the paintbrush feel like on the glass?
- Was it easy or difficult to paint glass? Why?

Variations

- Paint 'frames' or borders, such as curtains or portholes, onto windows to accompany a theme.
- Add related craft to a painted glass surface.
- Paint onto plastic sheeting to form decorated partitions in the classroom.

Cross-curricular activities

- Investigate weather conditions, including the appropriate clothing, shelter and food associated with them.
- Investigate the properties of water, such as sinking and floating and capacity.
- Practise using water for cleaning or drinking.
- Pretend it is a rainy day and dress up in raincoats. Sing 'rainy day' songs.

Resources

- red, yellow, green and blue powder paint
- paintbrushes (flat, wide, large, round)
- white paper
- liquid starch (see teachers notes)
- coloured paper scraps
- scissors
- lime green card for mounting
- newspaper
- glue

Indications:

Skills, techniques, technologies and processes

- Combines paints on the page using a wide paintbrush to create a semi-mixed effect.
- Uses a wet paintbrush to 'pick up' and apply powder paint.

Responding, reflecting on and evaluating visual arts

- Makes appropriate additions to a textured background to create a familiar image.

Inspiration

- Collect flowers and observe the diversity of colour.
- Dissect flowers to find the pollen.
- Smear pollen on paper to note the consistency.
- Brainstorm other substances with similar qualities, such as powder and flour.
- Investigate what happens to powder when blown into the air. Note how it is suspended in the air.

Instructions

Step 1

Prepare a solution of green powder paint. (See page x.) The paint should be thick enough to cover the page but thin enough to have some translucent areas. Using a wide, flat paintbrush, apply the powder paint, trying to keep all brush strokes in the same direction across the page to create a background for the artwork. The final result should have visible brushstrokes and incorporate darker and lighter areas, rather than one flat colour. Allow the paint to dry completely.

Step 2

Make a mixture of liquid starch. (Directions for homemade commercial-strength liquid starch can be found on page x.) Use a wide paintbrush to spread the liquid starch thickly over the painted page. Liquid starch is a clear-drying adhesive suitable for lightweight gluing tasks.

Step 3

Dip a large, round paintbrush into water and then into the dry powder paint so that the brush picks up the dry paint particles. Dab the powder particles over the page while the liquid starch is still wet to create a background of thick 'pollen' in the air. Some particles will become a thick paint when in contact with the liquid starch on the page. The students can make a special effect by placing the 'pollen' on the page or brushing very gently to spread the pollen particles around. Small brushstrokes can give the illusion of the pollen floating on the breeze if the brushstrokes are all in the same direction.

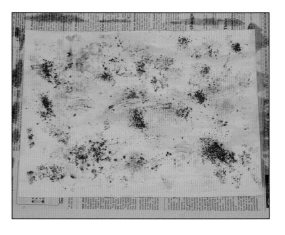

Pollen painting

Step 4 Cut out flower and butterfly shapes to glue to the page. Alternatively, provide the students with precut shapes (these are available commercially) to add to their artwork to create a spring garden scene. Glitter can also be added while the liquid starch is still wet. Mount on a lime green background on a pink display wall.

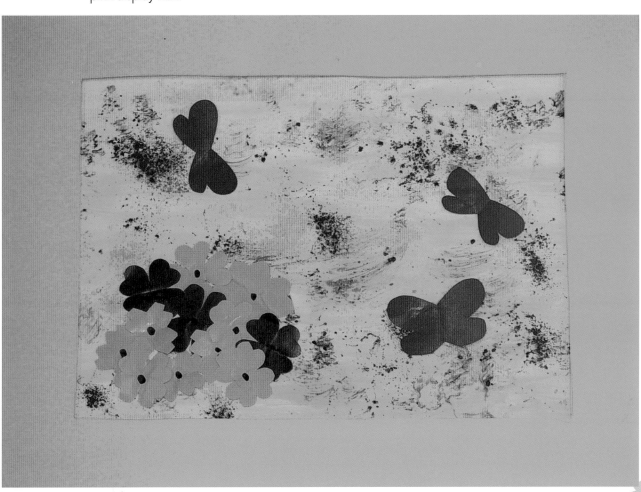

Reflection questions

- Does the powder paint represent pollen and the diversity of colours among flowers well?
- What happened to the powder paint when it was sprinkled onto the starch glue?
- How could the picture be further enhanced? What could be added?

Variations

- Cut large coloured flowers and use the same technique to create colourful pollen in the centre of each flower.
- Use the technique on white paper to create wrapping paper. Add glitter to enhance.
- Sprinkle powder paint in patterns to create simple sunset pictures.

Cross-curricular activities

- Investigate how plants grow and reproduce. Find out what pollen is for and how it is carried to other locations.
- Complete 'spring' activities, such as growing seedlings, visiting a farm with baby animals or having a big clean-up.
- Classify or sequence flowers or leaves collected according to a criterion such as colour, shape or size.

Resources

- white art paper
- drinking straw
- red card for mounting
- yellow paint
- red marking pen
- food colourings/dye
- aluminium foil
- scissors
- paintbrush
- newspaper

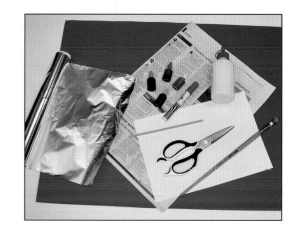

Indications:

Skills, techniques, technologies and processes

- Applies dye randomly and 'pulls' the liquid into shapes.
- Draws outlines around shapes.

Responding, reflecting on and evaluating visual arts

- Imagines that the simple shapes they create represent jelly beans.
- Invents a suitable jar as a mount.

Inspiration

- Display a jar of jelly beans. Discuss the colours and shapes.
- Allow the students to sample one and describe the taste.
- Discuss favourite confectionery, their type, shape and colour.

Instructions

Step 1

On a white piece of paper, make small blobs of dye in different bright colours randomly all over the page. Art paper will give the best results as it is slightly absorbent and the food colouring will not run as readily, allowing the students to 'pull' their blobs into shapes. The simplest way to apply the blobs is to use food colouring with a dropper dispenser. Alternatively, edicol dyes can be used and applied using the tip of a round paintbrush or a cotton bud.

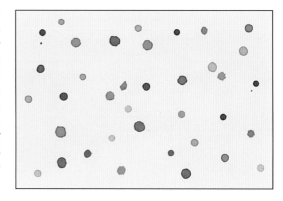

Step 2

Using the end of the paintbrush (not the brush end), drag the wet blobs into jelly bean shapes. Imaginative students might attempt to drag their blobs into other confectionery shapes and should be encouraged to do so. In some cases, the blobs will mix together. The artwork will look most effective if some blobs are left their original colour; however, mixing some blobs will be an interesting experiment for the students and should not be discouraged. When dry, the mixed blobs will produce some interesting patterns and colours.

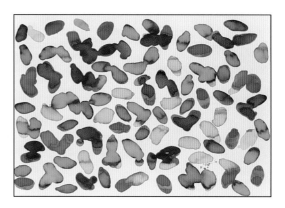

Step 3

Use a small dry paintbrush with full-strength acrylic paint to paint the gaps between the jelly beans. Be aware that the dye colours will run when they come into contact with moisture. Therefore, this painting will need to be done very carefully. Alternatively, the students can use a felt-tipped pen or colouring pencils to colour the gaps.

When dry, use a thick marking pen to trace around each of the jelly beans and redefine their shapes.

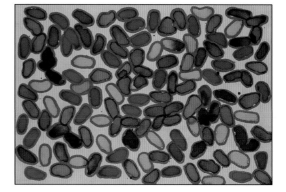

J▢lly bean j▢r

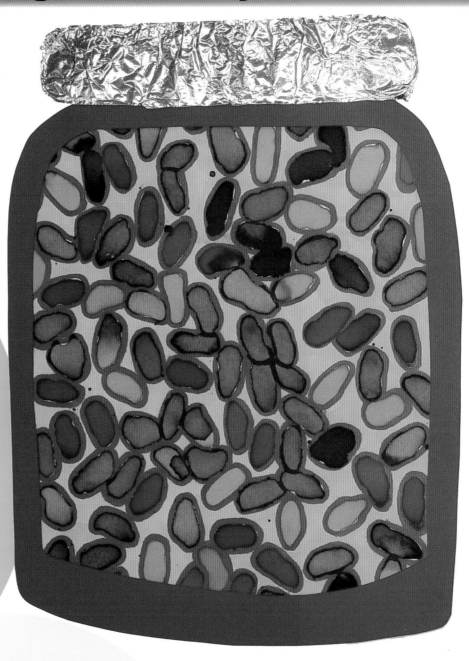

Step 4

Design and create a border in the shape of a jar. Students may require assistance to cut the internal boundary of the frame. Shape a section of foil over the top lip of the 'jar' to create a lid. Display on a royal blue wall as if sitting on a shelf.

Reflection questions

- Do your jelly beans look yummy?
- What kinds of shapes did you make by 'dragging' the dye?
- What happened when the droplets touched?
- What colours look most attractive?
- What shape did you choose for your jar? What other shapes could the jar have been?

Variations

- Experiment with different paint consistencies (more or less watery), using the straw to move the paint around the page.
- Students attempt to blow an ink blob into a tree shape using a straw.
- Use only two primary colours to illustrate how the colours mix to create a new 'secondary' colour.

Cross-curricular activities

- Investigate healthy and unhealthy foods.
- Experiment with wet jelly beans to see the food colouring they contain. Find out other foods that contain artificial colouring.
- Play counting and sorting games using colourful jelly beans as counters
- Use jelly beans as units for measuring mass and capacity.

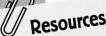
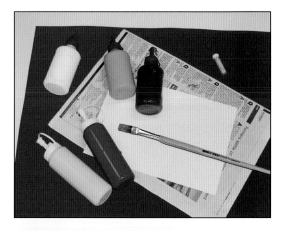

Indications:

Skills, techniques, technologies and processes

- Combines paints on the page using a wide paintbrush to create a semi-mixed effect.
- Applies paint with squeeze bottles

Responding, reflecting on and evaluating visual arts

- Attempts to create an image of icicles using a specified technique.
- Understands that sometimes colours do not need to be mixed completely.

Inspiration

- Make colourful iceblocks in the freezer for the students to eat. Discuss the properties of ice.
- Look at pictures of icicles hanging from window frames or over-hanging rocks.
- Discuss how the dripping nature of water may cause icicles to form.

Instructions

Step 1

Squirt blue and white paint in stripes down the length of the page. Use a wide paintbrush to spread and cover the page with paint so that the colours are partially mixed on the page. The final result should be darker and lighter areas of blue in patches down the length of the page. The effect will be enhanced if all of the brushstrokes are also run vertically down the page.

Step 2

Squirt large amounts of white paint to create white 'puddles' at the top of the page. Drop smaller amounts of blue and purple paint into the puddles. Some puddles should be larger than others.

Step 3

Lift the paper at the 'puddle' end and allow the paint to flow down the page to create long, white icicles. The purple and blue paint will form streaks down the crystals as they flow. If the blue and purple areas are lost in the flow, the students may need to re-apply small amounts further down the length of the icicles. Similarly, if the flow stops short, add more white paint to assist movement.

Note: If salt is added to the paint at a 1:1 ratio, the paint will flow more readily and the icicles will take on a sparkly effect when dry.

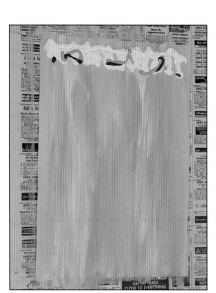

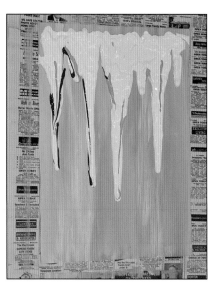

Icicle crystals

Step 4

When the paint is still wet, sprinkle the icicles with silver glitter. When dry, display side by side with the icicles made by other students in the class along a windowsill to create a wintery scene. Alternatively, mount on a striking 'cool-coloured' background.

Reflection questions

- How do your icicles look? What could help them look more life-like?
- Did your icicles drip easily? Did you do anything special to make them drip? Do you think any other techniques could have worked better?

Variations

- Make stalagmites and stalactites in a cave setting using the drip method.
- Add small amounts of water to assist paint flow.
- Make a lava flow for a volcano model.
- Put dripping candle wax on a candle template for Christmas, using the drip method.

Cross-curricular activities

- Investigate the defining characteristics of winter.
- Brainstorm to list cold things and provide samples for the students to view and touch.
- Find out about cold places such as Antarctica, the lifestyle of people temporarily there, and the animals they share the icy landscape with.

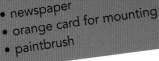

Resources

- good quality art paper
- water
- coloured paints
- sponge
- bowls
- newspaper
- orange card for mounting
- paintbrush

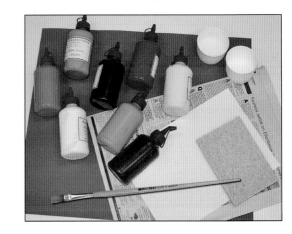

Indications:

Skills, techniques, technologies and processes

- Applies paint to a wet surface.
- Uses a paintbrush to move paint around a wet surface.

Responding, reflecting on and evaluating visual arts

- Appreciates that paint reacts differently to wet and dry surfaces and creates different effects.
- Respects the limitations of working on an unpredictable wet surface.

Inspiration

- Add drops of food colouring to a glass jar of water and observe how the colour disperses into the water in patterns.
- Predict what will happen when paint is added to a watery surface.
- Look at the way colours mix to produce new colours.

Instructions

Step 1

Prepare the work surface with newspaper. Use a wet sponge to completely saturate a sheet of absorbent art paper. It is important to use good quality paper for this activity to avoid soggy artworks tearing.

Step 2

Drop a blob of paint onto the wet paper. Note how the paint reacts to the moisture and 'bleeds' across the page. Use a paintbrush to push the paint around in patches and long fingers. Watch it spread. Encourage the students to think about how they will use the colours they have to make patterns. Discuss the types of pictures this kind of painting might suit; for example, sunsets or underwater scenes.

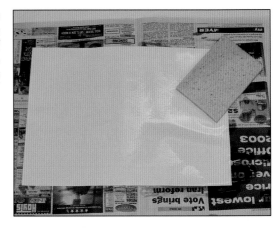

Step 3

Use the same colour on other parts of the page. Add other colours in between to create a swirling mixture of paint colours. It is important not to over-mix the colours or to allow them to flow too freely into one another. If it becomes difficult to spread the paints at any stage, additional water can be brushed onto the page to improve the 'bleeding' effect. If the page becomes 'muddy', a sponge can be used to remove excess moisture. Allow the artwork to dry completely on a flat surface.

Wet paper painting

Step 4 When dry, the wet paper painting can be used as a background for other artwork or collages, cut up to make shapes for displays, used to cover books or simply mounted on card and displayed.

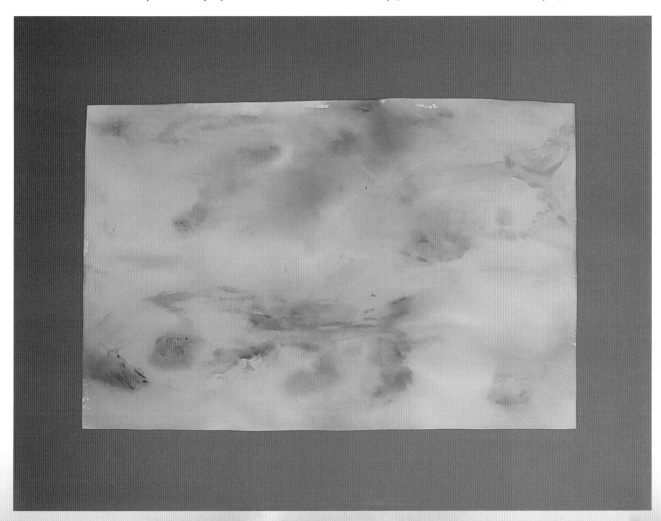

Reflection questions

- How did the paint react with the wet paper surface?
- Were the colours bright? How would you describe them?
- What did you do to blend the colours?
- Did you make any colours you didn't like?
- What pictures do you think this type of painting would suit?

Variations

- Use the wet paper technique to create a sunset sky. Cut shapes from black paper to make silhouettes.
- Add blue paint to wet paper to create a swirling 'underwater' background on which to mount a fish collage.
- Use the same technique with different types of paper and compare the results.

Cross-curricular activities

- Investigate where paper comes from and how it is made.
- Make paper by recycling scraps of used card and paper. Write letters to one another on the paper.
- Conduct an experiment to discover things that absorb water.
- Provide free water play so that students can experiment with things that will float and sink.
- Discuss the ways in which water is good for our body.

Resources
- newspaper
- fluorescent paints
- thick paintbrushes
- toothbrushes
- fluorescent card for mounting
- white art paper
- streamers and confetti (optional)

Indications:

Skills, techniques, technologies and processes

- Creates long splatter stripes across a page by flicking a loaded paintbrush.
- Produces a speckled effect on paper by flicking the bristles of a toothbrush loaded with paint.

Responding, reflecting on and evaluating visual arts

- Enjoys the freedom of creating 'flicked' patterns.
- Appreciates the messy nature of flick-painting and respects the need to create in a controlled manner.

Inspiration

- Encourage the students to share 'splashing' experiences.
- Students imagine a painting produced by splashing. What techniques would they use to produce the painting?
- Prepare a large protected area for the students to demonstrate splattering techniques for their peers using water only.

Instructions

Step 1

Splatter painting is extremely messy and should be done on grassed areas if possible. Alternatively, cover a large area of ground with newspaper (at least one metre square). Ensure the artists and their assistants are wearing painting shirts or old clothes suitable for getting dirty.

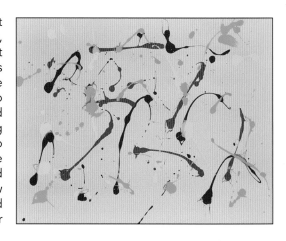

Step 2

Load a thick paintbrush with paint and, standing back from the page, flick the paint from the brush across it to create a thick, splattery stripe. This may need to be demonstrated for the students and the students allowed to practise the action using an unloaded brush several times before beginning their painting. Use the same colour to make three or four splatters and move to another colour. The students should be allowed to use as many or as few colours as they like and be encouraged to verbalise reasons for their colour choices. Allow the splatters to dry.

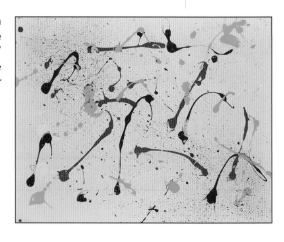

Step 3

Demonstrate how to use a toothtbrush to create a speckled splatter on the page. Allow the students to 'speckle' their own artwork using the same colours they used to make the splatter stripes.

Splatter painting

Step 4 When dry, choose a colour used in the painting as a mount. Display the work together with flashcards of descriptive words and phrases such as 'blobby splotches', 'splish-splash', and 'dib, dab, dob'. Add colourful streamers and confetti to the display. Alternatively, the students can draw an outline of a person and cut it out to make a 'Professor Messer'.

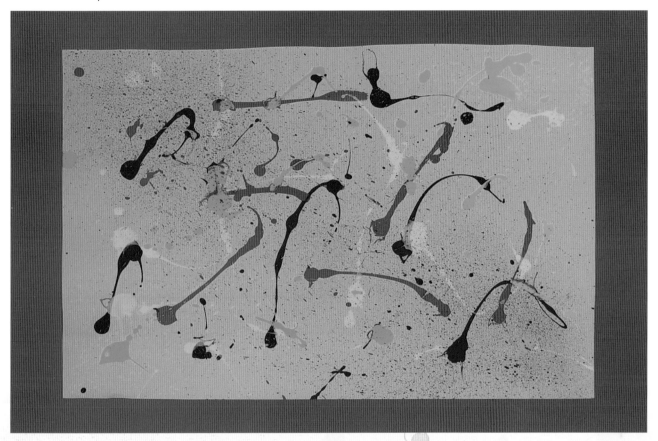

Reflection questions
- How did you go about making the 'splatter' prints?
- Was it messy? Is your painting messy?
- Did the splatters land where you had planned?
- What else could you have done or used to create the splatters?

Variations
- Make splatter prints by dropping a heavy, spongy ball onto the surface. A tennis ball works well.
- Dip a length of rope or string into paint and drop it onto the paper from a height. Drag the string across the page to make interesting patterns.
- Use squeeze bottles to drop small blobs of paint from a height onto coloured paper. Use many different colours and allow them to overlap to create a vibrant image.

Cross-curricular activities
- Brainstorm to write a list of words to describe rain.
- Use instruments to create the sounds of a splattery, rainy thunderstorm.
- Make a large 'splat' on a page and write a short story about a time when something went 'splat'.
- Provide a water play area and encourage the students to make the water plop, pour, splatter and squirt.

- fluorescent paint
- fluorescent yellow card for mounting
- thick white paper
- newspaper
- icing sugar (powdered sugar)
- water
- paintbrush
- container
- green/yellow marking pen

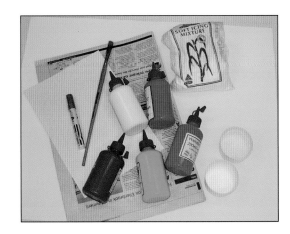

Indications:

Skills, techniques, technologies and processes

- Uses icing sugar mixed with water to create a unique effect with paint.

Responding, reflecting on and evaluating visual arts

- Enjoys watching paint react with a solution of icing sugar and water.
- Understands that paint reacts differently with different media to create unique effects.

Inspiration

- Look at pictures of different types of marbling or go on a nature walk to discover marbled patterns in nature.
- Students observe what happens to diluted paint or dye when it comes in contact with different cooking ingredients.
- Students taste and describe the icing sugar they will be using in their art.

Instructions

Step 1

Mix equal parts of icing sugar and water together to create a thin syrup.

Step 2

Use a thick paintbrush to completely saturate a sheet of absorbent art paper with the syrup. It is important to use good quality paper for this activity to avoid soggy work tearing. Drop a blob of slightly watered-down acrylic paint or mid-strength powder paint onto the wet sticky paper. Note how the paint reacts to the syrup and 'bleeds' into interesting patterns. Encourage the students to think about how they will use the colours they have to make a marbled pattern. Discuss pictures this effect might suit.

Step 3

Use the same colour on other parts of the page. Add other colours in between to create a swirling mixture of paint colours. It is important not to over-mix the colours or to allow them to flow too freely into one another. If it becomes difficult to spread the paints at any stage, additional water can be brushed onto the page to improve the 'bleeding' effect. Allow the painting to dry on a flat surface. The syrup may take some time to dry.

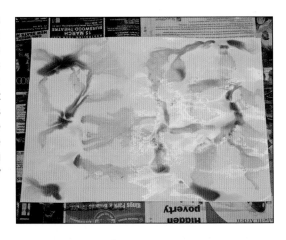

Icing sugar marbling

Step 4   Allow the painting to dry completely. If desired, use a green or yellow marking pen to trace a design among the marbled shapes. Mount on a bright background to accentuate the colours in the marbling.

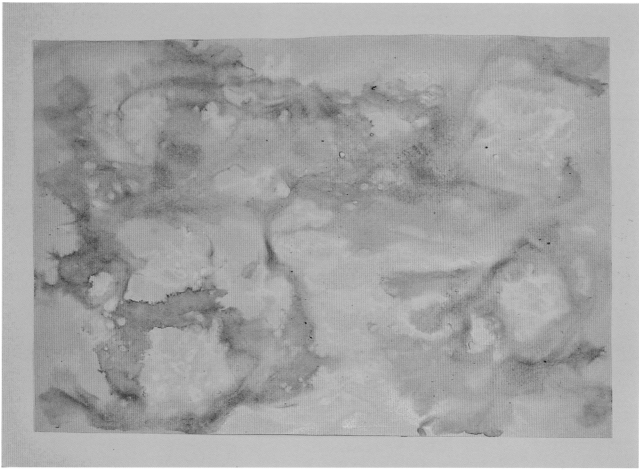

Reflection questions

- What happened to the paint when it came in contact with the icing sugar?
- Did the icing sugar make the kinds of patterns you imagined?
- Did you add any drawn lines to create images from the marbling? How did you use the icing sugar patterns to help you decide where to draw your design?

Variations

- Make marble cake or ice-cream by mixing different coloured mixtures together.
- Sprinkle jelly crystals onto a liquid starch surface and 'marble' the colours together to create a 'sweet'-smelling marbled picture.
- 'Marble' paper by taking a print of dye floating on a thick solution of liquid starch.

Cross-curricular activities

- Mix icing sugar with milk and butter to make an icing mixture. Students ice and decorate their own biscuits or cakes.
- Review dental hygiene and the effects of sugar on teeth.
- Sort a selection of foods and drinks according to whether or not it they have sugar in them.
- Follow step-by-step instructions to make a simple recipe containing sugar, such as pancakes.
- Write a simple sugary recipe.

Resources
- red paint
- fork
- everyday tools (comb, toothbrush, scrubbing brush)
- white paper
- newspaper
- black card for mounting
- wide paintbrush

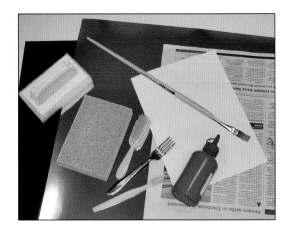

Indications:

Skills, techniques, technologies and processes

- Paints a surface thickly to prepare it for etching.
- Uses everyday objects as 'tools' to create patterns in thick paint.

Responding, reflecting on and evaluating visual arts

- Invents unique ways to make impressions on wet paint.
- Combines different types of etching to produce an original picture or pattern.

Inspiration

- Discuss what is meant by 'etching'.
- Brainstorm to find objects which could be used to make an impression in paint.
- Look at examples of etchings or carvings where special tools have been used to mark the surface.
- Encourage the students to bring household items from home that could be used to make interesting etchings.

Instructions

Step 1

Use acrylic paint or cornflour paint and a wide paintbrush to thickly cover a piece of paper. Instructions for how to make cornflour paint can be found on page x.

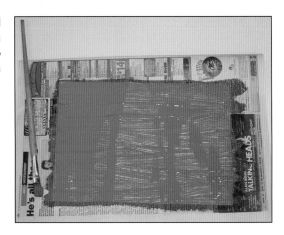

Step 2

Use a fork to demonstrate how everyday objects can be used as tools for making impressions on a painted surface. Students describe the type of impression or 'etch' the fork made and what a fork could be used to draw in the paint. Brainstorm a list of possible tools that could be used to create interesting patterns in paint. If possible, allow the students to bring in their own painting tools from home to use.

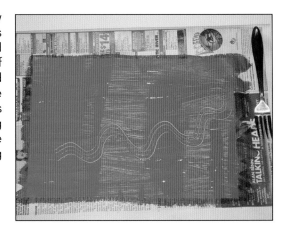

Step 3

Allow the students to experiment with the everyday tools they have chosen to use. The students can etch and repaint their paper to make a smooth new canvas to work on several times. When they are satisfied with the patterns or picture they have created, they can put their painting on a flat surface to dry.

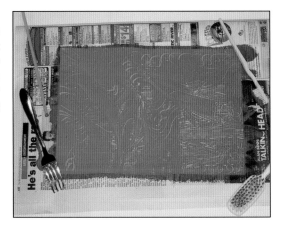

Etch painting

Step 4 For a striking result, use red paint and mount on a silver background against black. This activity can also be done directly onto aluminium foil, sprinkled with glitter and mounted on a black background for a metallic finish.

Reflection questions

- What household items did you use to make patterns in your paint?
- Describe some of the patterns you made.
- Were some more effective than others? Which do you think look the best? What do you think makes these patterns look good?
- Could you combine some of these etchings to make a picture? Describe how you would construct your picture.

Variations

- Paint onto coloured paper or card so that the etching will reveal the base colour.
- Paint onto aluminium foil and etch the wet paint surface away carefully to reveal a silvery, shiny design.
- Etch patterns or pictures into cakes of soap, clay or blocks of polystyrene.
- Use fingers to etch patterns into thick cornflour paint.

Cross-curricular activities

- Investigate different types of tools and how they are used.
- Provide an imaginative play corner where the students can role-play different occupations and the tools they use.
- Play a game of charades where the students have to 'guess the tool'.
- Students write a short personal profile outlining the type of work they think they might like to do when they grow up. Include the tools they would need and the reasons why they would like to do that type of work.

Glossary – Painting

bleed	a term used to describe the manner in which a liquid medium spreads
boundary	a dividing line or limit
carving	a medium shaped by cutting
collage	a picture made from pieces of paper, cloth or other materials pasted onto paper or board
edicol	dye created from natural products, often in the form of powder
impressionism	a 19th century-style in which artists attempted to paint the fleeting effects of natural light with the bright, pure colours of the spectrum
interpretation	explain, translate, bring out the meaning of by artistic representation of performance
marbling	to create the look of marble; a mottled pattern of various colours
medium	a means or material used by an artist to produce work or art
modern art	twentieth century art; includes periods such as impressionism, post-impressionism, cubism, fauvism, expessionism, bauhaus, surrealism and futurism
open-ended	having no predetermined limit or boundary
primary colour	one of three base colours used to create all other colours – blue, yellow and red
random	happening or being done without a plan or purpose
secondary colour	colour produced when two base colours are mixed; for example, red and yellow mix to create the secondary colour orange
silhouette	an outline drawing filled with black like a shadow
solution	substance which is made up of one chemical, usually a solid, spread perfectly throughout another chemical, usually a liquid
supernova	a star that suddenly increases very greatly in brightness because of an explosion ejecting most of its mass
texture	the roughness or smoothness of a material
textured paint	paint which has been mixed with a second medium such as sand, salt or flour to create an interesting consistency
translucent	allowing some light to come through
vibrant	bright, lively and exciting
viscous	sticky, glutinous, semi-fluid

Useful websites

Artist and movements

National Gallery of Art	www.nga.gov
Impressionism	www.impressionism.org/
Art in context	www.artincontext.org/index.htm
The worldwide art gallery	www.theartgallery.com.au

Tools and Techniques

Colour museum	www.sdc.org.uk/museum/mus.htm
ArtLex on collage	www.artlex.com
The art of marbling	members.aol.com/marbling/marbling/

Art education

Early childhood art lessons	www.princetonol.com/groups/iad/lessons/early/early.html
The incredible art department	www.princetonol.com/groups/iad/

PRINTMAKING

Resources
- tray
- yellow and orange paint
- scissors
- glue
- yellow paper
- white art paper
- yellow card for mounting
- newspaper
- coloured paper scraps (optional)

Indications:

Skills, techniques, technologies and processes

- Uses hands to print.
- Combines hand prints to create flower shapes.

Responding, reflecting on and evaluating visual arts

- Enjoys using hands as a tool for applying paint.
- Thinks about how to position hand prints to create a desired image.

Inspiration

- Allow the students to fingerpaint with thick cornflour-based paint to familiarise them with the way paint feels and behaves.
- Look at different types of flowers, noting the shape and number of petals.
- Make prints using hands and feet. Hold hands in different positions to create different-shaped prints.
- View *Sunflowers* by Van Gogh (1888).

Instructions

Step 1

Prepare a work area with layers of newspaper or plastic sheeting. Ensure the students' clothing is well protected.

Pour yellow and orange paint onto a shallow tray. Paint thickened with cornflour is appropriate but not essential for hand and finger painting activities. See the cornflour paint recipe on page x.

Allow the students to use their fingers and hands to mix the paint on the tray and make a hand print on a blank sheet of paper. Encourage the students to make the print towards the top of the page.

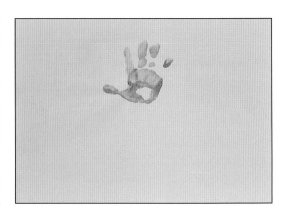

Step 2

Repeat this process, so that each hand print joins the previous to form a radiating flower pattern, using fingers as petals. Print two or three 'finger' flowers using as many sheets of paper as required.

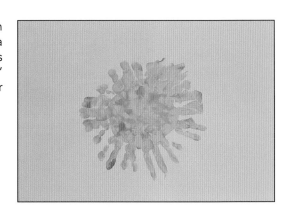

Step 3

Tear pieces of yellow coloured paper, crepe paper, or tissue paper and crumple into small balls. These balls will become the pollen in the flower centres. Glue the crumpled balls into the centre of each flower, covering most of the 'palm' sections of the prints.

Cut around the general perimeter of each flower, leaving a narrow margin of white paper as a border for each.

Finger flowers

Step 4

Glue each of the flowers onto a yellow background. If desired, glue leaves, a plant pot or extended petals from coloured paper squares. Garden insects such as butterflies and beetles might also be added to provide a colour contrast.

Reflection questions

- How did the paint feel in your hands?
- Was your hand print the same shape as your hand? How was it different?
- What flower parts did your fingers make? What part of the flower did your palm make?
- What colour did you choose for your flower? Was this a good choice?

Variations

- Make prints of real flowers.
- Combine hand prints to enhance other pictures; for example, to make a rooster's tail, leaves on a tree, or fur on an animal.
- Make prints using other body parts or prints of the hand in different positions to create imagined creatures. Enhance with felt-tipped pens when dry.
- Make fingerprint creatures or fingerprint flowers.

Cross-curricular activities

- Investigate things that grow. Find out what plants need to stay alive and to grow.
- Grow a punnet of annuals for the students to care for and observe.
- Use a display of brightly coloured flowers to reinforce knowledge of colours.
- Investigate ways pollen is carried from one plant to another.
- Find out about fruit that develops from flowers.

Resources

- tray
- corncobs
- sponges
- white art paper
- dark green card for mounting
- yellow and green paint
- glue
- newspaper
- green crepe paper
- foam roller

Indications:

Skills, techniques, technologies and processes

- Uses food items to create unusual prints.
- Uses a sponge roller lengthways to create a corn stalk.
- Adds collage materials to enhance a print.

Responding, reflecting on and evaluating visual arts

- Enjoys the challenge of producing a picture that represents a real-life object.
- Appreciates that unusual prints can be made from everyday objects.

Inspiration

- Brainstorm a list of vegetables. Discuss which might make unusual prints.
- Cut a variety of vegetables in different ways to create interesting cross-sections.
- Discuss how the choice of colour affects what the final print might resemble.
- Discuss the types of pictures that could be made using vegetable shapes.

Instructions

Step 1

Prepare a work area with newspaper or plastic sheeting. Ensure the students are wearing protective clothing.

Look at pictures of cornstalks or view corn growing if possible. Discuss the shape of the stalk and the way the ears of corn grow out from the stem. Pour green paint on a tray. 'Load' a foam roller with the green paint. Turn the roller sideways so that it makes a vertical line print rather than rolling the roller lengthways. Print several vertical lines above each other to create a cornstalk. Add short stalks coming from either side as a 'growing point' for the corn cobs. Using the same printing technique, add two or three curved leaves to the stalk. Allow to dry.

Step 2

Pour yellow paint onto a tray. Roll a corncob in the paint and carefully make a print at each 'growing point' on the stalk by rolling the corncob slightly to print several rows of kernels. Allow to dry.

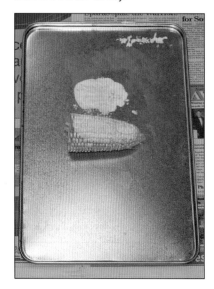

Step 3

Cut long leaf shapes from green crepe paper and cut in half as shown. Bunch the wide end of the leaf shape together and glue down securely to appropriate points at the base of each corncob, so that the leaf partially covers the corn. Allow to dry.

Corncob prints

Step 4

Loosely fold back the crepe paper leaves so that the corncob prints can be clearly seen. Do not press the folds down. Rather, allow the leaves to stand out from the picture to add a new dimension to the print. Mount on a dark green background to display.

Reflection questions

- What vegetables did you use? Did they suit the picture you were trying to create?
- What colours did you use? Could you have used any other colours? How would that have changed your picture?
- What other vegetables could you have used? What could you have created with them?
- How did you apply paint to the vegetable?
- Could you have done this another way?

Variations

- Use simple carving tools to carve shapes into potatoes to print.
- Print fruits such as oranges and apples cut in half.
- Experiment with a single vegetable to create many different cross-section prints.
- Use vegetable prints to create a healthy 'vegie person'.
- Use vegetables to print borders, wrapping paper or cards.

Cross-curricular activities

- Use vegetable prints to create or extend patterns.
- Cut a carrot at several angles and compare the cross-sections.
- Cook and eat vegetables. The students can cut vegetables to add to a vegetable soup or stew.
- Investigate foods that are good for our bodies. Discuss foods that are good for certain things; for example, carrots for good vision.

Resources
- lime green card for mounting
- vegetation
- toothbrush
- newspaper
- white art paper
- green, yellow and blue paint
- tray
- paintbrush

Indications:

Skills, techniques, technologies and processes

- Uses objects from their natural environment to create interesting prints.
- Uses two different printmaking techniques to describe the shape and boundaries of a leaf.

Responding, reflecting on and evaluating visual arts

- Selects objects from nature that are suitable for making prints.
- Describes the criteria by which they assess whether or not their print was a success.

Inspiration

- Introduce the students to silhouettes. Students attempt to recognise objects from their silhouettes.
- Students search the local natural environment for plants with unusual leaf shapes.
- Discuss the different colours found in leaves at different times of the year.
- Observe the patterns formed by veins within leaves.

Instructions

Step 1

Prepare a work area with newspaper or plastic sheeting. Ensure the students are wearing protective clothing.

Pour blue and yellow paint onto a tray big enough to allow the leaves to lie flat across the surface. Use a paintbrush to spread and slightly mix the colours together to create variations of green. Carefully place the leaf on the surface of the mixed paint and press down lightly. Peel the leaf from the paint surface and carefully place paint side down onto a sheet of paper. Do not remove the leaf. Repeat this process for any additional leaves. It is best to work from the largest to the smallest leaf or item to be printed. Again, leave the leaves on the page.

Step 2

Load a toothbrush with paint from the tray. Carefully run a finger across the bristles of the brush so that the paint flicks across the printed page. Cover the page with a spatter effect. The leaves sitting on the page will mask areas where the spatter cannot reach and thus create a boundary for each of the leaves.

Step 3

Carefully remove the leaves from the page to reveal the two different kinds of print. It is important that the spatter printing takes place immediately to ensure the leaves do not dry onto the surface of the print. Allow the print to dry.

Nature prints

Step 4   Mount the print on a lime green background. Alternatively, mount several leaf prints together against a background of rainforest colours and add unusual and brightly coloured animals and insects such as cassowaries, poison arrow frogs and blue triangle butterflies to the display to make a collage.

Reflection questions

- Did the leaves you chose print well? Why did you choose the leaves you did?
- How did you apply paint to the leaves? Was this effective?
- Did you have any difficulties printing the leaves you chose? If yes, how did you overcome these problems?
- Are you pleased with the finished product?
- What might you do differently next time?

Variations

- Use autumn leaf colours on orange or earth-coloured paper.
- Use dead leaves, sand, pebbles and bark to make a collage to add an extra dimension to your prints.
- Use leaf prints to create a plant or tree picture.
- Make prints of bark, flowers or other 'once-living' things.

Cross-curricular activities

- Investigate changing seasons.
- Put white daisies in water with food colouring to demonstrate how plants take up water. (The daisies will turn the colour of the dye in the water.)
- Investigate things that live in forests or rainforests.
- Investigate insects that use leaves for food and/or shelter.
- Sample edible leaves, such as lettuce leaves and snow pea shoots.

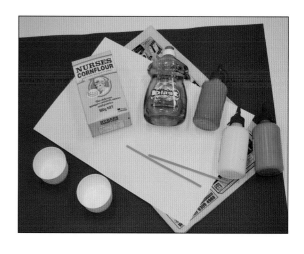

Resources

- detergent
- newspaper
- small containers
- drinking straw
- white art paper
- pink card for mounting
- acrylic or cornflour paint

Indications:

Skills, techniques, technologies and processes

- Blows bubbles into a paint solution to create a bubbly surface for printing.
- Takes a print from a surface by placing the surface to be printed on top of the print subject.

Responding, reflecting on and evaluating visual arts

- Describes their prints as 'bright' or 'pastel'.
- Identifies the transfer of patterns from the print subject to the print itself.

Inspiration

- Allow the students to use detergent and bubble wands to blow bubbles. Observe the way they float on the breeze.
- Students engage in water play with bubble bath or detergent. Allow them to froth the water using beaters or with running water.
- Observe the shapes and sizes of the bubbles as they join and burst.

Instructions

Step 1

Prepare a work area with newspaper or plastic sheeting. Ensure the students are wearing protective clothing.

Pour brightly coloured acrylic paint into a small container such as a yogurt tub. Add a squirt of detergent and a small amount of water to thin the paint slightly. (Cornflour paint also works well for this activity.) Using a straw, blow directly into the paint mixture to create bubbles. Continue to blow until the bubbles rise above the top of the container. You may need to add more detergent if you are finding this difficult to achieve.

Step 2

While the bubbles are still above the lip of the container, take a sheet of white paper and lower it down carefully over the bubbles. Lift the paper away and place on a sheet of newspaper, print side up to dry. A bubbly pattern will remain where the paper came in contact with the paint bubbles.

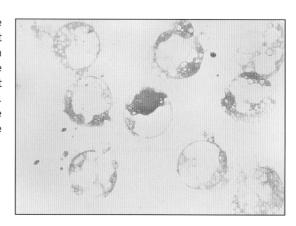

Step 3

Make several bubble prints in the same colour across the page. Repeat using other bright colours. The vividness of the colours will depend upon the type of paint used. Using cornflour-based paint will produce brighter colours, while acrylics will generally produce pastel bubble prints.

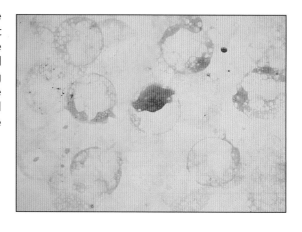

Bubble prints

Step 4 Mount against a background that matches the brightness of the bubble prints produced. For example, use a pastel background with a pastel print. If displaying the prints en masse, add balloons and other 'bubbly' textures such as bubble wrap or polystyrene beans to create a visual and tactile display.

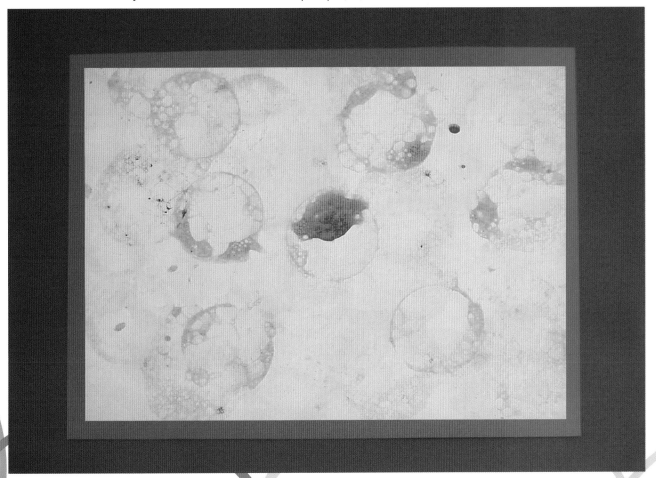

Reflection questions
- How did you make the bubbles?
- What shapes did the bubbles make on the page? Were they all round?
- What colours did you use?
- Did you make a picture from your bubble print shape? What pictures could you make from a bubble print?
- How would you describe the prints you made?

Variations
- Blow single bubbles using a thick detergent and paint mix. Chase the bubble and catch it on a blank sheet of paper. Repeat many times to create a different kind of bubbly picture.
- Trace around groups of printed bubbles to create bath monsters. Add detail such as faces, arms and legs.
- Overlap many different coloured bubbles to combine and create new colours.

Cross-curricular activities
- Investigate things that float and sink.
- Make frothy milk shakes.
- Discuss personal hygiene, especially using soap to keep clean.
- Use detergent and sponges to squeeze and make froth. Clean down dolls or toys from the 'home' corner.
- Discuss germs that live in dirty things and how they can make you sick.

Indications:

Skills, techniques, technologies and processes

- Makes linear prints by rolling marbles coated in paint across a page.
- Controls the direction of the marbles by tilting the printing tray.

Responding, reflecting on and evaluating visual arts

- Attempts to 'fill the page' by thinking about the way the tray should be tilted and balanced in order to move the marbles.
- Accepts the erratic nature of marble printing and that some forms of printing cannot be fully controlled.

Inspiration

- Students look at the tracks left by a variety of living things, from dogs to snails.
- Students predict the path that objects or creatures might leave.
- Show the students some marbles and give them the opportunity to try to balance and roll them around on a flat surface.

Resources

- white paper
- newspaper
- marbles or other small spheres
- fluorescent paints
- fluorescent card for mounting
- small containers; e.g. eggcups
- tray

Instructions

Step 1

Prepare a work area with newspaper or plastic sheeting. Ensure the students are wearing protective clothing.

Line a tray with paper. The sides of the tray will need to be high enough to contain the movements of a marble rolling inside it.

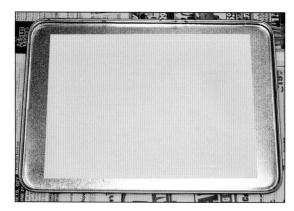

Step 2

Pour fluorescent paint into a small container such as an eggcup. Drop a marble or small sphere into the paint so that it is completely coated. Alternatively, roll the marble through paint on a palette until it is covered.

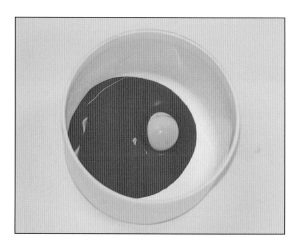

Step 3

Retrieve the marble and drop it onto the tray lined with paper. Move the marble around on the tray by tilting the tray backward and forward. Attempt to control the movements of the marble in order to use all the space on the page. The marble may need to be recoated several times during this process. When finished, students should wash their hands and the marble.

Prepare several other eggcups with different coloured fluorescent paints and, one by one, apply each paint colour using the same printing process.

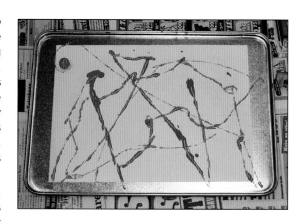

Marble pattern

Step 4

Carefully remove the sheet from inside the tray and lie it flat to dry. Mount against a bright fluorescent background. Interesting patterns can also be created using this technique by rolling several marbles at one time, however, be careful to choose only two or three colours which will mix well, to avoid an ugly mess.

Reflection questions

- Were you able to control the paths your marbles made? Were there any patterns that kept occurring?
- What colours did you choose? Did they become mixed? Did this make your picture better or worse?
- What could you use your marble print for?
- What else could you use to make interesting paths?

Variations

- Students slide or roll other 3-D shapes to create path prints.
- Use sponges dipped in paint to make 'snail trails'.
- Use fluorescent paint on boldly coloured card to make marble prints.
- Students draw lines on the page to be printed and use a single marble dipped in paint to attempt to trace the line.
- Use nuts or seed pods in place of marbles.

Cross-curricular activities

- Play simplified games of marbles.
- Create a class display of special marbles.
- Introduce the students to other traditional playground games such as skipping rhymes and hopscotch.
- Investigate animal prints and trails. Match prints to animals.
- Discuss situations where people might need to 'track' footprints or trails.

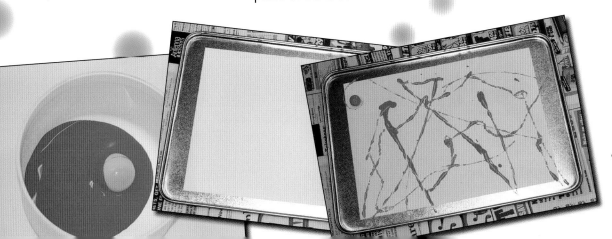

Resources
- clay
- acrylic paint
- newspaper
- envelopes
- white paper
- sponge
- tray
- carving tools
- felt-tipped pens

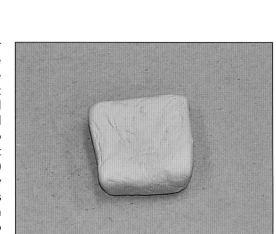

Indications:

Skills, techniques, technologies and processes

- Forms clay into a stamp shape.
- Successfully etches a planned design.
- Produces a print using his or her own stamp.

Responding, reflecting on and evaluating visual arts

- Chooses a design that is representative of their personality or interests.
- Evaluates the effectiveness of their clay stamper.

Inspiration

- Students play with modelling media such as clay, plasticine or playdough to give them experience in rolling balls, making ropes and shaping surfaces.
- Look at a range of different stamps.
- Discuss the types of things depicted on stamps.
- Students share something special they might use to represent themselves on a stamp.

Instructions

Step 1

Prepare a work area with newspaper or plastic sheeting. Ensure the students are wearing protecting clothing. Provide the students with clay modelling equipment including modelling boards and carving tools. (A heavy board covered in calico works well and will absorb excess moisture in the clay and prevent the clay sticking to the work surface.) Carving tools can be the commercially produced variety or simply toothpicks or even old, sharpened pencils. Form a small piece of clay into a square stamp shape. Begin by rolling the clay into a smooth ball. The best way to produce the flat surfaces of the sides is to simply drop a ball of clay onto a flat surface to create flattened sides. Repeat this for each surface until the clay takes on the shape of a rectangular prism.

Step 2

Think about your own personality, likes and dislikes, hobbies and interests and imagine a design that represents you in some way. It may simply be a smiling face if you are a happy person. Use the carving tools to etch your design into one of the flat surfaces of your clay stamp. Once the carving is complete and any excess clay particles have been removed, drop the etched surface onto the board again to flatten out any ridges that might alter the print.

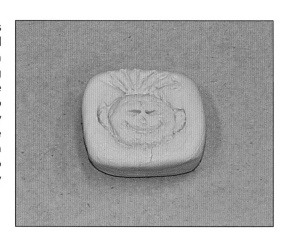

Step 3

Press the stamp into paint and make several prints on a sheet of paper. Clean the stamper with a paper towel in between colours. Do not wash it in water.

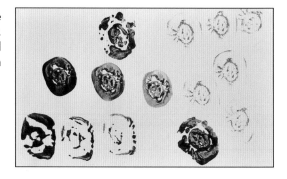

Clay stamps

Step 4

After a practice run on paper, use your stamper to make prints on the corners of several envelopes. Address your envelope and write a letter to put inside. Keep your stamper and use it as your personal logo to label your books, other artwork and special projects.

To Amy From Amelia

To Dad From Abbey

To Grandy From Peter

Reflection questions

- What did you draw on your stamp to represent yourself?
- Describe what the clay felt like to model.
- Did your clay stamp make a clear print? Could you have made your print clearer? How?
- Did you use your stamp on envelopes? Who could you send stamped letters to?

Cross-curricular activities

- Write letters, attach stamps and post at the local post office.
- Create a class letterbox and encourage the students to write letters to one another.
- Write letters to Santa or thank you letters to visiting guests.
- Provide stamps of the letters of the alphabet and an ink pad. Use them to write or 'stamp' their names.
- Find out why stamps are needed to send mail.

Variations

- Make other stamps using soft materials such as vegetables or soap instead of clay.
- Make clay stamps with the students' initials and print onto workbooks.
- Engrave pictures into wider slabs of clay stand print using more than one colour.
- Provide the students with stamps and coloured ink pads and allow them to decorate cards.

Resources

- red and yellow greasy crayons
- red and yellow paint
- textured fabric scraps
- tray
- sponges
- white paper
- newspaper
- hard roller
- blue card for mounting
- scrap paper

Indications:

Skills, techniques, technologies and processes

- Takes rubbings of material scraps to show their texture.
- Makes prints of material scraps to show their texture.

Responding, reflecting on and evaluating visual arts

- Identifies the materials with textures most suitable for making rubbings and prints.
- Compares the clarity of the rubbings to the prints.

Inspirations

- Compare the textures of a variety of different fabrics. Students attempt to describe them in their own words.
- Discuss the types of clothes that could be made from each of the fabrics.
- Students practise holding the fabric taut while they make their rubbings. Allow them to work in pairs to do this, if necessary.

Instructions

Step 1

Prepare a work area with newspaper or plastic sheeting. Provide a wide selection of fabrics. Describe the texture of each fabric. Identify those with the most pronounced texture which would produce the best print or rubbing. Experiment on scrap paper, using greasy crayons, by making rubbings of each fabric. Choose the fabrics with the most interesting rubbings to include in an artwork. Rub each of these fabrics onto a fresh sheet of paper using red and yellow crayons.

Step 2

Ensure the students are wearing protective clothing. Pour red and yellow paint onto sponges in a tray. Place a piece of fabric onto the sponges so that it is covered by a thin coating of paint. Avoid a thick coating of paint as this will prevent clear printmaking.

Step 3

Carefully lift the fabric onto the page where the rubbings have been made. Use a hard roller to roll over the surface of the fabric. You may need a helper to hold the fabric firmly in place while you roll it to avoid moving it around and smudging the print. Repeat this process for the other textured fabric scraps used in the rubbings.

Step 4   Allow the print to dry and mount against bright blue card. These prints look great when cut into squares and mounted side by side into a patchwork quilt of fabric textures, leaving a narrow margin of blue between each of the printed squares.

Reflection questions

- Did you make some interesting fabric rubbings? Which do you like the best?
- Did you have any difficulties creating the rubbings?
- What fabrics made the best prints?
- Were the prints similar to the rubbings? Which were clearer?

Variations

- Use fabric rubbings as a background texture for other artworks or collages.
- Use different media for rubbings, such as greasy crayons, fluorescent crayons, charcoal, pastels, lead or coloured pencils.
- Students investigate and rub other textured surfaces and compare the rubbings that result.
- Cut garment shapes from rubbed or printed paper.

Cross-curricular activities

- Discuss the types of clothing used in different environments and climates.
- Students match items of clothing such as shoes, socks or gloves.
- Allow the students to practise using pegs to 'hang out washing' in an imaginary play corner.
- Provide students with dress-up clothing, play dressing-up games or wear costumes while telling short stories.

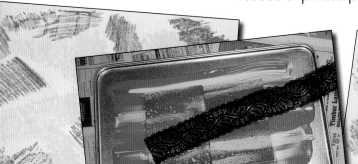

Resources
• red and black card for mounting
• black and red paint in 'squirt' bottles
• white paper
• scissors
• strong glue
• newspaper

Indications:

Skills, techniques, technologies and processes

- Creates a symmetrical print by folding wet paint.
- Attempts to apply paint in an insect shape using squeeze bottles.

Responding, reflecting on and evaluating visual arts

- Suggests how their paint could be applied in order to create the print they anticipate.
- Suggests how their paint could be altered to create a different print.

Inspiration

- Demonstrate how folding a page in half creates a symmetrical shape.
- Students suggest things found in nature that are symmetrical.
- Allow the students to make several attempts to create symmetrical blob shapes to become familiar with how paint behaves when squashed.

Instructions

Step 1

Prepare a work area with newspaper or plastic sheeting. Ensure the students are wearing protective clothing. Look at pictures of insects such as ants or beetles. Note their symmetry and think about how a folded print might produce the same image. Where would most paint need to go? Where would less paint need to be applied?

Use squirt bottles to apply black and red paint in the general shape of an insect, exactly in the middle of the page. Be careful not to apply too much paint as this will result in paint overflowing from the sides of the paper and the shape of the insect being lost. Paint should be applied very sparingly for this activity.

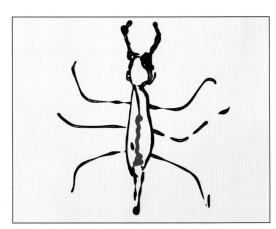

Step 2

Fold the paper in half while the paint is still wet so that the fold line runs down the middle of the insect. While the paper is still folded, cut around the perimeter of the shape leaving a narrow white paper margin. Discard the cut-away paper.

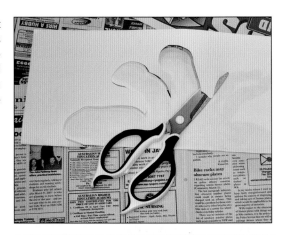

Step 3

Open out the print to reveal the symmetrical insect shape you created. Place on a flat surface to dry.

Insects blots

Step 4 When the print is dry, add detail if desired such as antennae, extra legs or a proboscis. Mount the cut-out print on red paper or card and display against a black background.

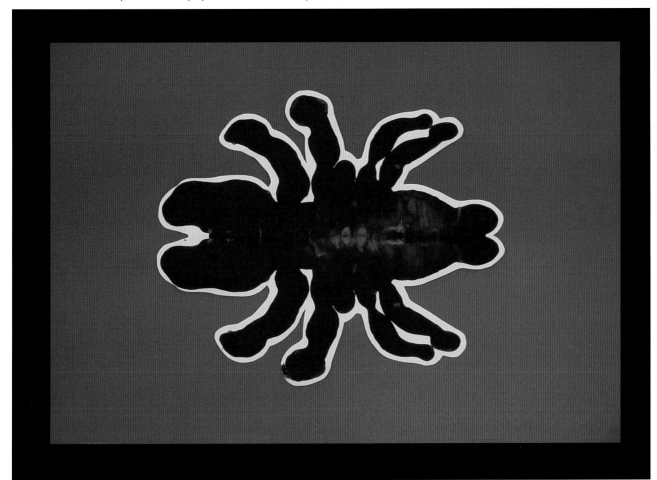

Reflection questions

- What kind of insect were you trying to create? Did it turn out the way you expected?
- Could you have applied more or less paint?
- Did you plan how you would try to make a symmetrical insect? Describe how you went about it. Would you do it differently if you made another symmetrical print?

Variations

- Students use a number of colours to create a butterfly. Add details such as legs or antennae using a felt-tipped pen.
- Students paint their name on one half of a sheet of paper and fold it in half to create a symmetrical pattern. They can then use other colours to paint the new shapes they created when the print was made.

Cross-curricular activities

- Conduct a playground search for insects. Give the students information to help them distinguish insects from other 'creepy-crawlies'.
- Provide an ant farm for the students to maintain and observe over time.
- Find out the life spans of flying insects.
- Sing songs such as 'Shoo fly' and 'Incy wincy spider'.
- Investigate 'safe' and 'unsafe' creepy-crawlies.

Resources

- several different-sized old shoes
- fluorescent pink, green and purple paint
- tray
- sponges
- white paper
- newspaper
- pink and fluorescent green card for mounting
- glue

Indications:

Skills, techniques, technologies and processes

- Creates prints using the soles of shoes.

Responding, reflecting on and evaluating visual arts

- Compares naturally occurring prints to those generated by artists.
- Appreciates that art can be created using everyday objects as inspiration.

Inspiration

- Make footprints in wet sand.
- Go on a footprint discovery tour to discover the tracks of other creatures.
- Compare the treads on the shoes of the students in the class. Look for similarities and differences among the treads. Describe the patterns of the treads.
- Discuss why we need tread on our shoes.

Instructions

Step 1

Find two or three different old shoes with interesting tread on the soles. Prepare a work area with newspaper or plastic sheeting. Ensure the students are wearing protective clothing. Pour fluorescent paints in several colours into a tray so that the edges of the colours are touching. Lay the sole of one of the shoes across the coloured paints in the tray.

Step 2

Lift the shoe out of the paint tray and carefully place it onto a large sheet of paper. Roll the shoe from toe to heel to make sure the entire surface of the sole has been printed. Carefully lift the shoe off the paper to reveal a sole print.

Step 3

Repeat the printing process using each of the shoes to cover most of the page. Consider how you will best fill the page. Attempt to alternate where the colours will fall on the page as you make each print. Allow the prints to dry.

'Sole' prints

Step 4   When dry, mount the 'sole' print against a fluorescent background to display. Sole prints can also be used to create linear patterns or 'tracks' along long sheets of butchers' paper. Alternatively, attempt to create the prints of animals by using other printing materials to create their tracks.

Reflection questions

- What kinds of shoes did you use? Why did you choose these shoes? How would you describe their treads?
- Did the shoes make the print you imagined? Can you tell which print belongs to which shoe?
- What colours did you choose to make your prints? Why did you think those colours would look good?

Variations

- Make rubbings of tyre treads.
- Make tracks using a pair of shoes.
- Make mini-animal prints using fingerprints, or craft stick prints.
- Cut out printed footprints and tape them to the floor to show a pathway through the classroom.
- Make footprints in wet clay. Dry the clay and paint.
- Make painted footprints with bare feet.

Cross-curricular activities

- Investigate different kinds of transport.
- Graph how the students travel to school.
- Construct things with wheels.
- Count by twos to count the wheels on trucks and trains.
- Look at different types of shoes for different occasions. Match shoes to the activities they suit.
- Put on walking shoes and go for a walk.

Indications:

Skills, techniques, technologies and processes

- Draws an 'invisible' pattern using candle wax.
- Uses a roller to paint a bubble wrap surface.
- Carefully uses bubble wrap to print a regular pattern.

Responding, reflecting on and evaluating visual arts

- Enjoys 'discovering' a hidden pattern through printmaking.
- Assesses the success of their 'discovery' based on the clarity of the hidden design.

Inspiration

- Recall things you've discovered. Discuss what it means to discover something.
- Talk about what invisible ink might do.
- Prepare several drawings in 'invisible ink' (wax) to paint over with a 'wash' (very runny ink or dye) and discover the invisible image.
- Demonstrate the pattern made by bubble wrap. Discuss why invisible lines would need to be quite wide when printing over the top with bubble wrap.

Resources

- candle
- bubble wrap
- blue paint
- silver and black card for mounting
- tray
- sponge roller
- hard roller
- newspaper
- white paper

Instructions

Step 1

Using a white candle, draw a picture or design onto a sheet of white paper. The design should be very simple with the lines drawn thickly, tracing over each line several times. Take care to note where the patterns have been drawn so as not to overlap accidentally.

Step 2

Prepare a work area with newspaper or plastic sheeting. Ensure the students are wearing protective clothing. Pour a watered-down solution of blue paint (about the consistency of full-cream milk) onto a tray and completely cover a sponge roller with the paint. Roll the roller back and forth several times to get an even spread of paint across the roller. Roll the paint onto the bubbly (raised) side of a sheet of bubble wrap.

Step 3

Turn the bubble wrap over and gently lie the paint side down on top of the paper with the candle wax design. Use a hard roller to roll over the top of the bubble wrap to ensure even printing. Carefully lift the bubble wrap from the printed surface to reveal the hidden design.

Bubble wrap discovery prints

Step 4   Allow the print to dry and mount on silver against a black background. Mount a series of 'mystery' pictures for viewers to 'discover' the image hiding within the bubble wrap print.

Reflection questions

- What was your mystery picture?
- What could you have done to make your mystery picture clearer?
- What kind of pattern did the bubble wrap make?
- Was it easy to see your mystery picture once you had made your print?

Variations

- Use other textured surfaces to print and reveal a hidden picture. Kitchen sponges, corrugated card and pieces of carpet or textured fabric work well.
- Write messages in wax and paint a wash over them to reveal the secret message.
- Drip liquid wax onto a sheet of paper to create a raised surface for taking a rubbing, or print it.

Cross-curricular activities

- Write letters to one another in 'invisible ink'.
- Make a list of 'amazing discoveries' for the students to add to and refer to.
- Play hide and seek, treasure hunts, memory games and guessing games.
- Brainstorm things that hide in the garden. Use a magnifying glass to discover some tiny things that hide in the garden.

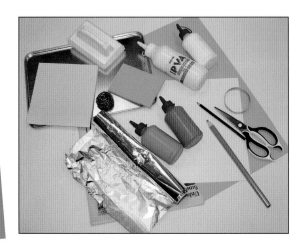

- egg ring or round biscuit/cookie cutter
- kitchen scourers (e.g. steel wool) and wipes
- orange, blue and white paint
- aluminium foil for mounting
- tray
- newspaper
- white paper
- scissors
- glue
- brown pencil or crayon

Indications:

Skills, techniques, technologies and processes

- Uses household sponges and scourers to create interesting prints.

Responding, reflecting on and evaluating visual arts

- Compares and matches scourers to their prints, based on texture and pattern observations.
- Identifies and gives reasons for preferred printmaking objects.

Inspiration

- Provide a wide variety of scourers, cloths and sponges to handle and explore in a tub of water.
- Describe the texture and properties of each of the scourers.
- Discuss 'washing up' experiences. Role-play or pretend to wash up using different scourers. What needs to be washed? What scourers will you use for each item?
- Attempt to match prints to the scourers that made them.

Instructions

Step 1

Use a brown crayon or coloured pencil to draw outlines of 'dirty' plates, cups, saucers, cutlery and pots and pans onto a large sheet of white paper.

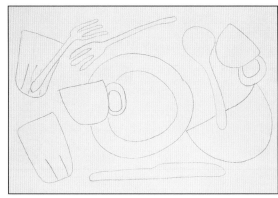

Step 2

Prepare a work area with newspaper or plastic sheeting. Ensure the students are wearing protective clothing. Pour orange paint onto a tray and select one of the scourers to make a print on the sheet with the drawings of dirty dishes. Dab the scourer onto the page, being careful not to move it to avoid smudging.

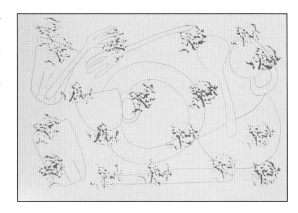

Step 3

Pour blue paint onto a tray and select another scourer to print in the same way. Overlap the prints to create brown areas where the orange and blue paint combine. Allow the prints to dry, then darken the outline of the crockery and cutlery.

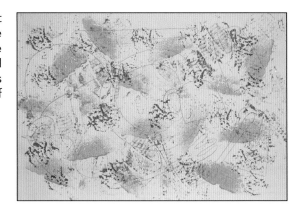

Scrubber prints

Step 4   Mount the prints inside a sink shape made from aluminium foil. Use an egg ring or cutter dipped in white paint to represent bubbles in opposite corners of the sink.

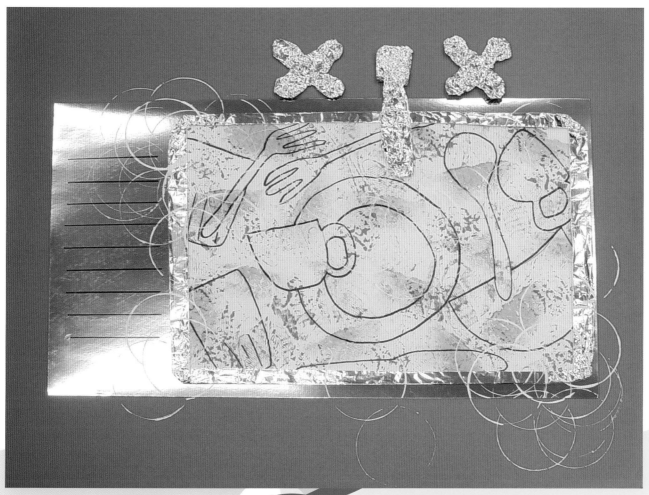

Reflection questions
- Which scourers created the most interesting prints?
- Do the plates in your 'sink' look dirty?
- Did you make your artwork look like a kitchen sink?
- How did you make bubbles around your sink? Do they look like real bubbles?

Cross-curricular activities
- Role-play household cleaning duties.
- Write a short story about a child who never cleaned up and created a huge mess.
- Review personal hygiene and the need to keep clean to avoid getting sick.
- Provide a large tray of water with detergent in it. Allow the students free discovery play to make bubbles, and 'clean' plastic crockery. Students can use a tea towel to dry up when they are finished.

Variations
- Use scourers to make prints inside the boundaries of an animal shape. Use an appropriate colour to create 'fur' prints over the animal's body.
- Wipe paint over a surface using a scourers to create swirling or wiggly prints.
- Cut sponges into simple shapes to print with. For example, print a traffic jam using a car shape or a colourful garden using a flower shape.

Resources

- yellow, orange, black and white paint
- large grey paper or card
- tray
- sponge roller
- newspaper
- black card for mounting
- feathers
- faux fur offcuts
- black marking pen
- pencil
- sponges

Indications:

Skills, techniques, technologies and processes

- Attempts to replicate the textures of feathers and furs by printing directly from the subject.
- Invents an animal incorporating both feathers and fur.

Responding, reflecting on and evaluating visual arts

- Decides upon the best positioning of feather and fur prints on their imaginary animal.
- Assesses the usefulness of feathers and fur as printmaking media.

Inspiration

- Look at pictures of animals with different body coverings.
- Provide scraps of furry and leathery fabrics and feathers for the students to handle. Discuss the types of prints they might make.
- Brainstorm ideas about an imaginary animal with both feathers and fur.

Instructions

Step 1

Imagine an animal that is composed of both feather and fur body coverings. Imagine where each body covering would sit on the animal. Picture it in your mind and then draw a simple outline of the animal you have invented onto a large sheet of grey paper or card. The outline should not include any feathers or fur – simply an outline. Trace with a black marking pen.

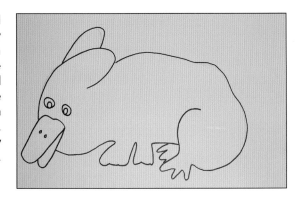

Step 2

Prepare a work area with newspaper or plastic sheeting. Ensure the students are wearing protective clothing. Pour 'feather–coloured' paints onto a tray and lay a feather on a paint surface. Alternatively, use a sponge roller to apply paint to the feather. Using a sponge will assist in helping the feather hold its shape better. Carefully lay the feather paint side down in a designated position on the outline of your animal. Repeat the process until all of the feathers required have been printed.

Step 3

Pour 'fur-coloured' paint onto a clean tray and press a swatch of faux fur into the paint. Again, using a roller will assist in achieving a better defined print. Press the fur onto the designated 'fur' sections of the outline. Complete any other details.

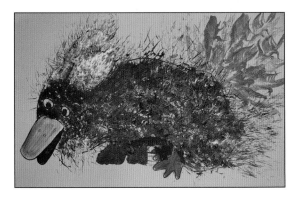

Step 4   Allow the prints to dry. If desired, glue feathers and faux fur onto some parts of the animal to create a more three-dimensional image and enhance the illusion created by the prints. Mount against a black background.

Reflection questions

- What kind of animal did you draw? Is it like any animal you know? Would you like to keep an animal like this as a pet? Why?
- Were your feather prints successful? Did they look like feathers or something different?
- Were the fur prints successful? How would you describe the prints you made with the fur?
- What colours did you use? Do they suit the animal?
- Are you happy with the animal you created? Did you enjoy printing it?

Variations

- Print with a variety of natural fibres such as cotton, wool and hessian.
- Create reptile prints using different parts of your hand.
- Use silver paint to print fish scales and create a fish.
- Use hand prints to create the feathers of a tail plume on a magnificent bird.
- Use a sponge to make interesting body covering textures. Cut animal shapes from the prints.

Cross-curricular activities

- Find out about native animals and their habitats.
- Discover the reasons why certain animals have the body coverings they do.
- Visit a wildlife park or zoo to see feathery and furry animals.
- Investigate and compare the body coverings of household pets.
- Find out about skin and what it does to help us survive.

Glossary – Printmaking

acrylic	synthetic fibres or substance
boundary	a dividing line or limit
charcoal	black porous residue of partly burnt wood
corrugated	wrinkled or folded material with strongly formed ridges
cross-section	transverse section of an object or drawing; for example, the circular surface created when a carrot is cut in half
erratic	unsteady and irregular in behaviour or movement
hessian (burlap)	strong, rough cloth often used to make sacks
linear	formed in a line
natural environment	surroundings which are found or formed by nature
palette	a thin board used by painters to mix colours on
pastel	a soft, pale colour or a soft chalk crayon or a drawing made with soft, chalky crayons
perimeter	the outside edge of a shape or area
print	to make copies of by pressing an inked surface onto paper or other material
rubbing	reproduced patterns or designs created by rubbing paper laid over a surface with a soft medium, such as chalk
silhouette	an outline drawing filled in with black, like a shadow
stamp	a engraved block or instrument used for making a mark on something
symmetry	the arrangements of the parts of something so that they are all balanced in size and shape
wash	a thin solution of paint and water used to paint rapidly over a surface

Useful websites

Artist and movements

The Metropolitan Museum of Art	www.metmuseum.org
Time line of art history	www.metmuseum.org/toah/splash.htm
Art in context	www.artincontext.org/index.htm
World printmakers	www.worldprintmakers.com/english/artists.htm

Tools and techniques

Dictionary of printmaking	www.philaprintshop.com/diction.html

Art education

Art junction	www.artjunction.org
Art education and ArtEdventures	www.alifetimeofcolor.com